YOUR

HOR

2016

LEO

YOUR PERSONAL HOROSCOPE 2016

LEO

23rd July–23rd August

igloobooks

igloobooks

Published in 2015
by Igloo Books Ltd
Cottage Farm
Sywell
NN6 0BJ
www.igloobooks.com

Copyright © 2015 Foulsham Publishing Ltd

Produced for Igloo Books by Foulsham Publishing Ltd, The Old Barrel Store,
Drayman's Lane, Marlow, Bucks SL7 2FF, England

Cover images: Thinkstock / Getty

HUN001 0715
2 4 6 8 10 9 7 5 3 1
ISBN 978-1-78440-585-4

This is an abridged version of material originally published
in Old Moore's Horoscope and Astral Diary.

Printed and manufactured in China

CONTENTS

Introduction   7

The Essence of Leo:
Exploring the Personality of Leo the Lion   9

Leo on the Cusp   15

Leo and its Ascendants   17

The Moon and the Part it Plays in your Life   31

Moon Signs   35

Leo in Love   39

Venus: The Planet of Love   43

Venus through the Zodiac Signs   45

Leo: 2015 Diary Pages   49

Leo: 2016 Diary Pages   71

Leo: Your Year in Brief   72

Rising Signs for Leo   157

The Zodiac, Planets and Correspondences   159

INTRODUCTION

Your Personal Horoscopes have been specifically created to allow you to get the most from astrological patterns and the way they have a bearing on not only your zodiac sign, but nuances within it. Using the diary section of the book you can read about the influences and possibilities of each and every day of the year. It will be possible for you to see when you are likely to be cheerful and happy or those times when your nature is in retreat and you will be more circumspect. The diary will help to give you a feel for the specific 'cycles' of astrology and the way they can subtly change your day-to-day life. For example, when you see the sign ☿, this means that the planet Mercury is retrograde at that time. Retrograde means it appears to be running backwards through the zodiac. Such a happening has a significant effect on communication skills, but this is only one small aspect of how the Personal Horoscope can help you.

With Your Personal Horoscope the story doesn't end with the diary pages. It includes simple ways for you to work out which zodiac sign was occupied by the Moon at the time of your birth, and what this means for your personality. In addition, if you know the time of day you were born, it is possible to discover your Ascendant, yet another important guide to your personal make-up and potential.

Many readers are interested in relationships and in knowing how well they get on with people of other astrological signs. You might also be interested in the way you appear to other people. If you are such a person, the section on Venus will be of particular interest. Despite the rapidly changing position of this planet, you can work out your Venus sign, and learn what bearing it will have on your life.

Using Your Personal Horoscope, you can travel on one of the most fascinating and rewarding journeys that anyone can take – the journey to a better realisation of self.

THE ESSENCE OF LEO

Exploring the Personality of Leo the Lion

(23RD JULY–23RD AUGUST)

What's in a sign?

What really sets you apart from the herd is your naturally cheerful tendencies and your ability to display a noble and very brave face to the world at large. Leos are big people, no matter what their physical size may be and it is clear that you could never be an 'also-ran'. Quite the reverse is usually the case because you are at the forefront of many ventures, ideas and enterprises.

Being a Leo brings quite a few responsibilities. For example, people tend to look up to you, which means you have to be on your best behaviour for a lot of the time. Not that this prevents you from showing a slightly mischievous face to the world on a regular basis. You are not given to worrying too much because you generally know how to get yourself out of any sort of difficulty with ease. It's true that you tend to face problems head-on – a natural extension of your rather courageous temperament. Sometimes this can get you into unnecessary scrapes, as can your tendency to pit yourself against the forces of nature, or social groups that you feel to be absolutely wrong in their intentions or objectives.

As a Leo you do recognise that you have a responsibility to others, particularly those types who are shyer than you, or individuals who just don't have the ability to look after themselves. With a smile and a shrug you are inclined to put a protecting arm around the whole world. In effect you are the perfect big brother or sister and take pride in the position you tend to gain in society. In a work sense you are capable and can very easily find yourself in a situation of responsibility. You don't worry about this and can make a fine executive in almost any profession. There's no doubt though that you are naturally best placed at the head of things.

THE ESSENCE OF LEO

It's true that you are inclined to do too much and that your levels of energy are far from inexhaustible. However, it's a love of life that counts for the most in your case, and nothing is going to prevent you from being the happy, sunny, freewheeling soul that represents the sign of Leo at its very best.

Leo resources

Your ruling planet is the Sun, the source of all heat, light and therefore life on the Earth. The Sun is fundamental to our very existence, and its primary importance at the centre of things is reflected in your nature. Unlike your brother sign, Aries, you display your Fire-sign tendencies in a more controlled manner and without the need to dominate to such a great extent. All the same your natural position is at the head of things and this is reflected in the resources you draw from the zodiac.

One of your greatest gifts is a natural tendency to look confident, even on those occasions when you might be quaking inside. It's amazing what a difference this makes because it more or less ensures that others will trust you and tend to follow your lead. Once they do you rise to the occasion in an admirable way because you don't want to let your followers down. In almost any situation that life could present, you will quite naturally take charge, and those around you are invariably happy that it should be so.

Most Leos are capable in a practical as well as a theoretical way but a hands-on approach probably works best. Leo leads from the front, which means having to keep fit and healthy. This is vital, but like the lion that your sign represents you can get rather lethargic and flabby if you don't keep in shape. Also like the lion you do have a tendency to appear lazy on occasions, but only usually when things are already running smoothly around you.

The professions chosen by Leos are many and varied. It isn't really the subject matter that is important, merely your ability to make an impression. At work, as well as in social situations, you can shine like the very Sun that rules you. Usually well liked and respected, you are in a position to utilise the popularity that comes your way in order to feather your own nest, as well as those of people around you. Domestically speaking you have a great love of home and family, though you might tend to stifle those you love a little on occasions.

Beneath the surface

'What really makes me tick?' A fair question, and one that members of many zodiac signs are constantly inclined to ask themselves – but not you. The fact is that you are not the deepest thinker around. This is not to suggest that you don't have lofty ideals or a very sound moral base to your behaviour. The reason that you probably are not one of life's natural philosophers is because you are a 'doer'. In the time it takes others to mull over any given situation you will have sorted it out and moved on to the next task. However, this is a natural skill that can be honed to perfection and depends in part on getting yourself interested in the first place.

Your boredom threshold tends to be quite low and you would soon feel fatigued if you were forced to remain in situations which meant doing the same thing time and time again. Your driving, sometimes impatient mentality does demand change, and you can become irritable and out of sorts if you don't find it.

Are you as confident as you often appear to be? The answer to that one has to be yes. The fact is that you quite often fail to bear in mind the possibility of failure. Of course this means that you are more disappointed than most when things do go wrong, but your very conviction often leads to success. Once you do get down in the dumps however, you can be a very sorry picture indeed. Fortunately, you have the mental and spiritual reserves to pick yourself up fairly quickly and to push forward once again.

In matters of love you are probably more reserved than you give the impression of being. All the same you know how to deal with relationships – that is until you start acting like a lion again. The over-protective quality of your animal sign is always a danger, and one that you need to control. Perhaps here we find the Achilles heel of Leo. It is quite common for you to experience a sense of jealousy, a fact that would make you more possessive than usual. You have to remember that it's fine to love, but impossible to 'own' another individual.

In the main you offer the world an exterior smile that reflects your genuine inner state. Truthfulness shows on your face, and is usually felt in your heart in equal proportion.

Making the best of yourself

To feel good and to make the right sort of impression, you have to look good too. Nobody goes to the safari park to see a moth-eaten lion. You can dress cheaply, but you have to cut a dash in some way. Drab colours definitely don't suit your personality, with bright oranges and yellows being the most favoured – a reflection of your Sun rulership. Once you are properly attired you tend to move forward positively through life. Most Leos are quite attractive people, mainly because the honesty, frankness and genuine courage of your personality has a habit of finding its way to the surface.

There is one line of Kipling's famous poem 'If' that springs to mind as an object lesson for Leo, this being 'And yet don't look too good, nor talk too wise'. It is quite possible for you to go over the top in your enthusiasm and even courage isn't same thing as foolhardiness. A little humility can go a long way, as can a determination to learn from people who know better than you do. Constantly knocking your head against the same brick wall isn't very productive, and can sometimes be avoided by simply showing a willingness to take advice. And it isn't as if people are unwilling to lend a hand. The Leo subjects who achieve the most in life have learned how to co-operate, though without feeling that they are having to relinquish the leading position in life that is so important to them.

In order for you truly to make the best of yourself you also need to be fit. Leos are inclined to have some problems associated with the heart and the circulatory system, so you need to exercise regularly and to avoid the sort of constant stress that can lead to longer-term health difficulties. To most Leos laughter is the best tonic of all.

The impressions you give

If we could all genuinely see ourselves as others see us, how much easier would be our interaction with the world at large? Yours may not be the most intuitive sign of the zodiac but you are perceptive enough to know when you are giving the right impression. If this fact is sometimes obscured it is at least easy for you to monitor when things are not going right. In turn this should result in a slight modification of your own personality to take account of circumstances.

If you have any specific problem in this direction it stems from the fact that you are not a natural philosopher. Doing is far more important than thinking to you, a truism that can sometimes be your downfall. More attention to detail and a better appraisal of others allow you to offer a much better impression of yourself.

Most people already find you sunny, warm, frank, free, delightfully outspoken and very brave. All you have to do to achieve real success is to build on the qualities you already possess and to make allowance for the fact that the world is full of individuals. You can't browbeat others into liking you, even though popularity is important to you. There will always be people who don't take to your personality and there really isn't much you can do about the situation.

A great advantage for you is that it isn't difficult for you to appear to know what you are talking about, even when you don't. You can gain extra skills on the way and should use the very real magnetism of your personality both to help the world and to improve your own situation. Few people would find you easy either to dismiss or to forget, which can be another very definite advantage in life.

A sense of proportion is sometimes important, as well as a defined purpose in your statements and actions. All in all you have most of the components that allow you to be popular. Build on these and your true Leo worth will be there for all to see.

The way forward

No sign of the zodiac typifies its planetary ruler more than your own sign of Leo. When you smile, the Sun comes out and your laughter is so infectious that even the hardest-hearted types would be likely to smile themselves. Add to this the fact that you typify the statement 'fools rush in where angels fear to tread' and you have a formidable combination at your disposal. It might be the case that you fail to take account of some of your actions, but a good-humoured and intelligent attitude to life also allows you to get out of scrapes as easily as you get into them.

Cultivate your tendency to stick up for the underdog and don't get yourself into a position in life that means you constantly have to pay lip service to people who clearly don't know what they are doing. You can't stand incompetence, arrogance, cruelty or oppression. Of course this is a fine attitude, but you can't put the world right on your own, so once again co-operation proves to be the key to success.

In a career sense you need to be doing something that constantly stretches you. Your boredom threshold is not high and with constant tedium can come a worrisome streak and a tendency to health difficulties. Variety in work is the spice of your life, together with an active and useful social life, which is also vitally important.

In matters of love you are sincere and ardent, though with a tendency towards being a little too possessive. Allowing others the freedom to go their own way means finding more happiness yourself and lifts the noble qualities of your nature to new heights. Leos are still more likely than people from other zodiac signs to find one important relationship in life and to stick with it. Part of the reason for this state of affairs is that you have a horror of failure and will persist, even when others fall by the wayside.

You may not be creative in the generally accepted sense of the word but you have a good eye for colour and enjoy cheerful surroundings. Practical and capable, you won't need to call on the services of experts too often, since Leos generally don't shy away from DIY chores.

Diet is vitally important because as a Leo you are inclined to put on weight readily. Exercise helps here and is something you revel in anyway. Use your natural talents to the full, defend the weak and fight oppressors and you can't go far wrong in your life. Most important of all, keep smiling. You are tremendous fun to have around.

LEO ON THE CUSP

Astrological profiles are altered for those people born at either the beginning or the end of a zodiac sign, or, more properly, on the cusps of a sign. In the case of Leo this would be on the 23rd of July and for two or three days after, and similarly at the end of the sign, probably from the 21st to the 23rd of August.

The Cancer Cusp – July 23rd to July 25th

You tend to take life at a slower pace than Leo when taken on its own. You are more sensitive and quieter by nature, with slightly less drive and enthusiasm and a less dynamic disposition. With a creative and generally aspiring nature, you draw from Leo the fearless qualities that are typical of the sign, but these only tend to show on those occasions when you feel very strongly about things. There is quite a contradiction between these two signs and therefore you have a tendency to show very different faces in different circumstances. This fact makes you slightly awkward to predict and you often shock people as a result. Just when the world thinks it has you pigeon-holed, off you go at a tangent, perplexing your relatives and friends all over again. Family members are very important to you and when your aspiring and lofty qualities show most it is often on their behalf. In matters of love you tend to be very loyal, and have the ability to mix very well with others, enjoying cheerful and original people as part of your social circle.

One area that needs particular attention is your health. Although generally more robust than you probably give yourself credit for, you get through a tremendous amount of nervous energy, much more than others may realise. You need to watch your diet very carefully and to avoid acidic foods, which can upset your stomach. Apart from this, however, you are virtually indestructible and have the capacity to work long and hard to achieve your objectives.

At work you do your best to be adaptable and are very good at managing others. The natural frustrations of Leo, when faced with opposition, are less accented in your case. You have the ability to get on well and should make a mark for yourself when happy with your lot. Few would find you overbearing or bossy, although at times you seem to lack some of the natural Leo confidence. Most important of all though – you are kind, generous, trusting and very good to know.

The Virgo Cusp – August 21st to August 23rd

Perhaps the greatest difficulty for people born under the influence of this cusp is in making themselves understood. You probably think that you are the least complicated person in the world, but that isn't the way others see you. Your nature is full of contradictions. On the one hand you are fanatically tidy, and yet you can work in a state of almost total chaos; you love to travel and yet, deep inside, you are a home bird; and you talk a great deal, but often with quiet confidence. To disentangle all these contradictions is as difficult for you as it is for anyone else, and so you may often not reach the level of self-confidence that you deserve.

You have most of the positive qualities associated with the zodiac sign of Leo and your lofty, aspiring, sunny disposition is usually well accepted. Beneath this, however, is a quiet and contemplative person, who needs moments alone to synthesise the many happenings in a busy life. Usually physically robust, you do tend to worry more than is good for you, frequently about matters that are not particularly important. Meditation suits you well, particularly the kind that has a physical aspect, as this satisfies your Leo qualities, too. With a nervous system that varies from day to day, it is important for you to be sure that you achieve the level of relaxation that is vital to your Virgoan qualities. For you this could be anything between a crossword puzzle and two weeks on a cruise ship. In social settings you enjoy a degree of variety and can manage quite well with new people, even though you often tend to stick to people with whom you are familiar.

It's always important for you to keep an open mind and you shouldn't allow negative thoughts to build up. Keeping busy makes sense, as long as you don't continually choose to burn the candle at both ends. The people who know you the best do find you difficult to understand, but they are inclined to love you all the more for that. The most important character trait for you to cultivate is optimism because the more cheerful you remain regarding the future, the greater is the effort you expound upon it.

LEO AND ITS ASCENDANTS

The nature of every individual on the planet is composed of the rich variety of zodiac signs and planetary positions that were present at the time of their birth. Your Sun sign, which in your case is Leo, is one of the many factors when it comes to assessing the unique person you are. Probably the most important consideration, other than your Sun sign, is to establish the zodiac sign that was rising over the eastern horizon at the time that you were born. This is your Ascending or Rising sign. Most popular astrology fails to take account of the Ascendant, and yet its importance remains with you from the very moment of your birth, through every day of your life. The Ascendant is evident in the way you approach the world, and so, when meeting a person for the first time, it is this astrological influence that you are most likely to notice first. Our Ascending sign essentially represents what we appear to be, while the Sun sign is what we feel inside ourselves.

The Ascendant also has the potential for modifying our overall nature. For example, if you were born at a time of day when Leo was passing over the eastern horizon (this would be around the time of dawn) then you would be classed as a double Leo. As such, you would typify this zodiac sign, both internally and in your dealings with others. However, if your Ascendant sign turned out to be a Water sign, such as Pisces, there would be a profound alteration of nature, away from the expected qualities of Leo.

One of the reasons why popular astrology often ignores the Ascendant is that it has always been rather difficult to establish. We have found a way to make this possible by devising an easy-to-use table, which you will find on page 157 of this book. Using this, you can establish your Ascendant sign at a glance. You will need to know your rough time of birth, then it is simply a case of following the instructions.

For those readers who have no idea of their time of birth it might be worth allowing a good friend, or perhaps your partner, to read through the section that follows this introduction. Someone who deals with you on a regular basis may easily discover your Ascending sign, even though you could have some difficulty establishing it for yourself. A good understanding of this component of your nature is essential if you want to be aware of that 'other person' who is responsible for the way you make contact with the world at large. Your Sun sign, Ascendant sign, and the other pointers in this book will, together, allow you a far better understanding of what makes you tick as an individual. Peeling back the different layers of your astrological make-up can be an enlightening experience, and the Ascendant may represent one of the most important layers of all.

Leo with Leo Ascendant

This is a breathless combination! The fact is that you are a go-getter of the first order, and there is virtually nothing in life that would prevent you from getting what you want. The problem here is that once you have it, you probably want something else. All in all you could end up like a dog chasing its own tail and so the first advice is to slow down and enjoy the journey a little more. Not that all of this makes you any less likeable, or indispensable, to a whole host of people. You smile much more often than you scowl and you won't make heavy weather of problems that would rock others back on their heels.

You are rather materialistic, and ultimate success probably means more to you than it should, but you can easily stop on your hectic journey to take note of those who have fallen by the wayside and give them a helping hand. If all that power is used for the good of humanity you might even become a living saint, except for the fact that you would be too busy to accept the honour. Be careful that you don't weigh yourself down with so many responsibilities that you fail to notice your progress, and travel as much as you can because this will certainly broaden your mind. Most people find you very attractive and fun to have around.

Leo with Virgo Ascendant

Here we have cheerfulness allied to efficiency, which can be a very
positive combination for most of the time. With all the sense of
honour, justice and bravery of the Leo subject, Virgo adds better
staying power through tedious situations and offers you a slightly
more serious view of life than we would expect from the Lion alone.
In almost any situation you can keep going until you get to your
chosen destination and you also find the time to reach out to the
people who need your unique nature the most. Few would deny
your kindness, though you can attract a little envy because it seems
as though yours is the sort of personality that everyone else wants.

Most people born with this combination have a radiant smile
and will do their utmost to think situations through carefully. If
there is any tendency to be foolhardy, it is carefully masked beneath
a covering of Virgoan common sense. Family matters are dealt with
efficiently and with great love. Some might see you as close one
moment and distant the next. The truth is that you are always on
the go and have a thousand different things to think about, all at
the same time. On the whole your presence is noticed, and you may
represent the most loyal friend of them all.

Leo with Libra Ascendant

Libra brings slightly more flexibility to the fixed quality of the Leo nature. On the whole you do not represent a picture that is so very different from other versions of the Lion, though you find more time to smile, enjoy changing your mind a great deal more and have a greater number of casual friends. Few would find you proud or haughty and you retain the common touch that can be so important when it comes to getting on in life generally. At work you like to do something that brings variety, and would probably soon tire of doing the same task over and over again. Many of you are teachers, for you have patience, allied to a stubborn core. This can be an indispensable combination on occasions and is part of the reason for the material success that many folk with this combination achieve.

It isn't often that you get down in the dumps, as there is generally something more important around the next corner and you love the cut and thrust of everyday life. You always manage to stay young at heart, no matter what your age might be, and you revel in the company of interesting and stimulating types. Maybe you should try harder to concentrate on one thing at once and also strive to retain a serious opinion for more than ten minutes at a time, although Leo does help to control any flighty tendencies which show up.

Leo with Scorpio Ascendant

A Leo with intensity, that is what you are. You are committed to good causes and would argue the hind leg off a donkey in defence of your many ideals. If you are not out there saving the planet you could just be at home in the bath, thinking up the next way to save humanity from its own worst excesses. In your own life, although you love little luxuries, you are sparing and frugal, yet generous as can be to those you take to. It's a fact that you don't like everyone and of course the same is true in reverse. It might be easier for you to understand why you dislike others than to appreciate the reverse side of the coin, for your pride can be badly dented on occasions. Scorpio brings a tendency to have down spells, though the fact that Leo is also strongly represented in your nature should prevent them from becoming a regular part of your life.

It is important for you to learn how to forgive and forget, and there isn't much point in bearing a grudge because you are basically too noble to do so. If something goes wrong, kiss the situation goodbye and get on with the next interesting adventure, of which there are many in your life. Stop-start situations sometimes get in the way but there are plenty of people around who would be only too willing to lend a helping hand.

Leo with Sagittarius Ascendant

Above and beyond anything else you are naturally funny, and this is an aspect of your nature that will bring you intact through a whole series of problems that you manage to create for yourself. Chatty, witty, charming, kind and loving, you personify the best qualities of both these signs, whilst also retaining the Fire-sign ability to keep going, long after the rest of the party has gone home to bed. Being great fun to have around, you attract friends in the way that a magnet attracts iron filings. Many of these will be casual connections but there will always be a nucleus of deep, abiding attachments that may stay around you for most of your life.

You don't often suffer from fatigue, but on those occasions when you do there is ample reason to stay still for a while and simply take stock of situations. Routines are not your thing and you like to fill your life with variety. It's important to do certain things right, however, and staying power is something that comes with age, assisted by the fixed quality of Leo. Few would lock horns with you in an argument, which you always have to win. In a way you are a natural debator but you can sometimes carry things too far if you are up against a worthy opponent. Confidence is not lacking and you go with ease through situations that would cause many people to give up.

Leo with Capricorn Ascendant

What really sets you apart is your endless patience and determination to get where you want to go, no matter how long it takes you to do so. On the way there are many sub-plots in your life and a wealth of entertaining situations to keep you amused. Probably somewhat quieter than the average Leo, you still have the capacity to be the life and soul of the party on those occasions when it suits you to be so. Energy, when allied to persistence, is a powerful commodity and you have a great need to take on causes of one sort or another. Probably at your best when defending the rights of the oppressed, you take the protecting qualities of Leo to greater heights than almost anyone else who is touched by the idealistic and regal qualities of the sign. If arguments come into your life, you deal with them quickly and, in the main, wisely. Like most Capricorn types, you take to a few individuals who will play a part in your life for years on end.

Being a good family type, your partner and children are extremely important and you will lavish the same patience, determination and ultimate success on their behalf that you do when dealing with more remote situations. The fact is that you do not know any other way to behave and you are at your best when there is some mountain to climb.

Leo with Aquarius Ascendant

All associations with Aquarius bring originality, and you are no exception. You aspire to do your best most of the time, but manage to achieve your objectives in an infinitely amusing and entertaining way. Not that you set out to do so, because if you are an actor on the stage of life, it seems as though you are a natural one. There is nothing remotely pretentious about your breezy personality or your ability to occupy the centre of any stage. This analogy is quite appropriate because you probably like the theatre. Being in any situation when reality is suspended for a while suits you down to the ground, and in any case you may regularly ask yourself if you even recognise what reality is. Always asking questions, both of yourself and of the world at large, you soldier on relentlessly, though not to the exclusion of having a good time on the way.

Keeping to tried and tested paths is not your way. You are a natural trail-blazer who is full of good ideas and who has the energy to put them into practice. You care deeply for the people who play an important part in your life, but are wise enough to allow them the space they need in order to develop their own personalities along the way. Most people like you, many love you, and one or two think that you are the best thing since sliced bread.

Leo with Pisces Ascendant

You are a very sensitive soul, on occasions too much so for your own good. However, there is no better advocate for the rights of humanity than you, and you constantly do what you can to support the downtrodden and oppressed. Good causes are your thing and there are likely to be many in your life. You will probably find yourself pushed to the front of almost any enterprise of which you are a part because, despite the deeper qualities of Pisces, you are a natural leader. Even on those occasions when it feels as though you lack confidence, you manage to muddle through somehow, and your smile is as broad as the day. Few sign combinations are more loved than this one, mainly because you do not have a malicious bone in your body and will readily forgive and forget, which the Lion on its own often will not.

Although you are capable of acting on impulse, you do so from a deep sense of moral conviction, so that most of your endeavours are designed to suit other people too. They recognise this fact, and will push a great deal of support back in your direction. Even when you come across troubles in your life you manage to find ways to sort them out, and will invariably find something new to smile about on the way. Your sensitivity rating is massive and you can easily be moved to tears.

Leo with Aries Ascendant

Here we come upon a situation in which Leo is allied with another Fire sign. This creates a character that could appear to be typically Aries at first sight and in many ways it is, though there are subtle differences that should not be ignored. Although you have the standard Aries ability for getting things done, many of the tasks you do undertake will be for and on behalf of others. You can be proud, and on some occasions even haughty, and yet you are also regal in your bearing and honest to the point of absurdity. Nobody could doubt your sincerity, and you have the soul of a poet combined with the bravery of a lion.

All of this is good, but it makes you rather difficult to approach, unless the person in question has first adopted a crouching and subservient attitude. Not that you would wish them to do so. It's simply that the impression you give and the motivation that underpins it are two quite different things. You are greatly respected, and in the case of those individuals who know your real nature, you are also deeply loved. But life would be much simpler if you didn't always have to fight the wars that those around you are happy to start. Relaxation is a word you don't really understand and you would be doing yourself a favour if you looked it up in a dictionary.

Leo with Taurus Ascendant

Oh dear, this can be rather a hedonistic combination. The trouble is that Taurus tends to have a great sense of what looks and feels right, whilst Leo, being a Cat, is inclined to preen itself on almost any occasion. The combination tends towards self-love, which is all too likely for someone who is perfect. But don't be too dispirited about these facts, because there is a great deal going for you in other ways. For a start you have one of the warmest hearts to be found anywhere, and you are so brave that others marvel at the courage you display. The mountains that you climb may not be of the large, rocky sort, but you manage to find plenty of pinnacles to scale all the same, and you invariably get to the top.

Routines might bore you a little more than would be the case with Taurus alone, but you don't mind being alone. Why should you? You are probably the nicest person you know! Thus if you were ever to be cast up on a deserted island you would people the place all on your own, and there would never be any crime, untidiness or arguments. Problems only arise when other people are involved. However, in social settings you are charming, good to know and full of ideas that really have legs. You preserve your youth well into middle age but at base you can tend to worry more than is good for you.

Leo with Gemini Ascendant

Many Gemini people think about doing great things, whilst those who enjoy a Leo Sun do much more than simply think. You have the intrepid qualities of Gemini, but you always keep a sense of humour and are especially good to be around. Bold and quite fearless, you are inclined to go where nobody has gone before, no matter if this is into a precarious business venture or up a mountain that has not been previously climbed. It is people such as you who first explored the world, and you love to know what lies around the next corner and over the far hill.

Kind and loving, you are especially loyal to your friends and would do almost anything on their behalf. As a result they show the greatest concern for you too. However, there are times when the Cat walks alone, and you are probably better at being on your own than would often be the case for the typical Gemini subject. In many way you are fairly self-contained and don't tend to get bored too much unless you are forced to do the same things time and time again. You have a great sense of fun, could talk to just about anyone and usually greet the world with a big smile.

Leo with Cancer Ascendant

This can be a very fortunate combination, for when seen at its best it brings all the concern and the natural caring qualities of Cancer, allied to the more dynamic and very brave face of Leo. Somehow there is a great deal of visible energy here but it manifests itself in a way that always shows a concern for the world at large. No matter what charitable works are going on in your district, it is likely that you will be involved in one way or another, and you relish the cut and thrust of life much more than the retiring side of Cancer would seem to do. You are quite capable of walking alone and don't really need the company of others for large chunks of the average day. However, when you are in social situations you fare very well and can usually be observed with a smile on your face.

Conversationally speaking you have sound, considered opinions and often represent the voice of steady wisdom when faced with a situation that calls for arbitration. In fact you will often be put in this situation and there is more than one politician and union representative who shares this undeniably powerful zodiac combination. Like all those associated with the sign of Cancer you love to travel and can make a meal out of your journeys, with brave, intrepid Leo lending a hand in the planning and the doing.

THE MOON AND THE PART IT PLAYS IN YOUR LIFE

In astrology the Moon is probably the single most important heavenly body after the Sun. Its unique position, as partner to the Earth on its journey around the solar system, means that the Moon appears to pass through the signs of the zodiac extremely quickly. The zodiac position of the Moon at the time of your birth plays a great part in personal character and is especially significant in the build-up of your emotional nature.

Your Own Moon Sign

Discovering the position of the Moon at the time of your birth has always been notoriously difficult because tracking the complex zodiac positions of the Moon is not easy. This process has been reduced to three simple stages with our Lunar Tables. A breakdown of the Moon's zodiac positions can be found from page 35 onwards, so that once you know what your Moon Sign is, you can see what part this plays in the overall build-up of your personal character.

If you follow the instructions on the next page you will soon be able to work out exactly what zodiac sign the Moon occupied on the day that you were born and you can then go on to compare the reading for this position with those of your Sun sign and your Ascendant. It is partly the comparison between these three important positions that goes towards making you the unique individual you are.

HOW TO DISCOVER YOUR MOON SIGN

This is a three-stage process. You may need a pen and a piece of paper but if you follow the instructions below the process should only take a minute or so.

STAGE 1 First of all you need to know the Moon Age at the time of your birth. If you look at Moon Table 1, on page 33, you will find all the years between 1918 and 2016 down the left side. Find the year of your birth and then trace across to the right to the month of your birth. Where the two intersect you will find a number. This is the date of the New Moon in the month that you were born. You now need to count forward the number of days between the New Moon and your own birthday. For example, if the New Moon in the month of your birth was shown as being the 6th and you were born on the 20th, your Moon Age Day would be 14. If the New Moon in the month of your birth came after your birthday, you need to count forward from the New Moon in the previous month. Whatever the result, jot this number down so that you do not forget it.

STAGE 2 Take a look at Moon Table 2 on page 34. Down the left hand column look for the date of your birth. Now trace across to the month of your birth. Where the two meet you will find a letter. Copy this letter down alongside your Moon Age Day.

STAGE 3 Moon Table 3 on page 34 will supply you with the zodiac sign the Moon occupied on the day of your birth. Look for your Moon Age Day down the left hand column and then for the letter you found in Stage 2. Where the two converge you will find a zodiac sign and this is the sign occupied by the Moon on the day that you were born.

Your Zodiac Moon Sign Explained

You will find a profile of all zodiac Moon Signs on pages 35 to 38, showing in yet another way how astrology helps to make you into the individual that you are. In each daily entry of the Astral Diary you can find the zodiac position of the Moon for every day of the year. This also allows you to discover your lunar birthdays. Since the Moon passes through all the signs of the zodiac in about a month, you can expect something like twelve lunar birthdays each year. At these times you are likely to be emotionally steady and able to make the sort of decisions that have real, lasting value.

MOON TABLE 1

YEAR	JUN	JUL	AUG	YEAR	JUN	JUL	AUG	YEAR	JUN	JUL	AUG
1918	8	8	6	1951	4	4	2	1984	29	28	26
1919	27	27	25	1952	22	22	20	1985	18	17	16
1920	16	15	14	1953	11	11	9	1986	7	7	5
1921	6	5	3	1954	1/30	29	28	1987	26	25	24
1922	25	24	22	1955	20	19	17	1988	14	13	12
1923	14	14	12	1956	8	8	6	1989	3	3	1/31
1924	2	2/31	30	1957	27	27	25	1990	22	22	20
1925	21	20	19	1958	17	16	15	1991	11	11	9
1926	10	9	8	1959	6	6	4	1992	1/30	29	28
1927	29	28	27	1960	24	24	22	1993	20	19	17
1928	18	17	16	1961	13	12	11	1994	9	8	7
1929	7	6	5	1962	2	1/31	30	1995	27	27	26
1930	26	25	24	1963	21	20	19	1996	17	15	14
1931	16	15	13	1964	10	9	7	1997	5	4	3
1932	4	3	2/31	1965	29	28	26	1998	24	23	22
1933	23	22	21	1966	18	17	16	1999	13	13	11
1934	12	11	10	1967	7	7	5	2000	2	1/31	29
1935	1/30	30	29	1968	26	25	24	2001	21	20	19
1936	19	18	17	1969	14	13	12	2002	10	9	8
1937	8	8	6	1970	4	4	2	2003	29	28	27
1938	27	27	25	1971	22	22	20	2004	16	16	15
1939	17	16	15	1972	11	11	9	2005	6	6	4
1940	6	5	4	1973	1/30	29	28	2006	26	25	23
1941	24	24	22	1974	20	19	17	2007	15	15	13
1942	13	13	12	1975	9	9	7	2008	4	3	1/31
1943	2	2	1/30	1976	27	27	25	2009	23	22	20
1944	20	20	18	1977	16	16	14	2010	12	12	10
1945	10	9	8	1978	5	5	4	2011	2	2/31	29
1946	29	28	26	1979	24	24	22	2012	19	19	17
1947	18	17	16	1980	13	12	11	2013	8	7	6
1948	7	6	5	1981	2	1/31	29	2014	27	25	24
1949	26	25	24	1982	21	20	19	2015	17	16	15
1950	15	15	13	1983	11	10	8	2016	4	4	2

TABLE 2   MOON TABLE 3

DAY	JUL	AUG	M/D	R	S	T	U	V	W	X
1	R	U	0	CA	CA	LE	LE	LE	LE	VI
2	R	U	1	CA	LE	LE	LE	VI	VI	VI
3	S	V	2	LE	LE	LE	VI	VI	VI	LI
4	S	V	3	LE	LE	VI	VI	VI	LI	LI
5	S	V	4	LE	VI	VI	LI	LI	LI	LI
6	S	V	5	VI	VI	LI	LI	LI	SC	SC
7	S	V	6	VI	LI	LI	LI	SC	SC	SC
8	S	V	7	LI	LI	LI	SC	SC	SA	SA
9	S	V	8	LI	LI	SC	SC	SC	SA	SA
10	S	V	9	SC	SC	SC	SA	SA	SA	SA
11	S	V	10	SC	SC	SA	SA	SA	CP	CP
12	S	V	11	SA	SA	SA	CP	CP	CP	CP
13	T	V	12	SA	SA	SA	CP	CP	AQ	AQ
14	T	W	13	SA	SA	CP	CP	CP	AQ	AQ
15	T	W	14	CP	CP	CP	AQ	AQ	AQ	PI
16	T	W	15	CP	CP	AQ	AQ	AQ	PI	PI
17	T	W	16	AQ	AQ	AQ	AQ	PI	PI	PI
18	T	W	17	AQ	AQ	AQ	PI	PI	PI	AR
19	T	W	18	AQ	AQ	PI	PI	PI	AR	AR
20	T	W	19	PI	PI	PI	PI	AR	AR	AR
21	T	W	20	PI	PI	AR	AR	AR	TA	TA
22	T	W	21	PI	AR	AR	AR	TA	TA	TA
23	T	W	22	AR	AR	AR	TA	TA	TA	GE
24	U	X	23	AR	AR	TA	TA	TA	GE	GE
25	U	X	24	AR	TA	TA	TA	GE	GE	GE
26	U	X	25	TA	TA	GE	GE	GE	CA	CA
27	U	X	26	TA	GE	GE	GE	CA	CA	CA
28	U	X	27	GE	GE	GE	CA	CA	CA	LE
29	U	X	28	GE	GE	CA	CA	CA	LE	LE
30	U	X	29	GE	CA	CA	CA	LE	LE	LE
31	U	X								

AR = Aries, TA = Taurus, GE = Gemini, CA = Cancer, LE = Leo, VI = Virgo,
LI = Libra, SC = Scorpio, SA = Sagittarius, CP = Capricorn, AQ = Aquarius, PI = Pisces

MOON SIGNS

Moon in Aries

You have a strong imagination, courage, determination and a desire to do things in your own way and forge your own path through life.

Originality is a key attribute; you are seldom stuck for ideas although your mind is changeable and you could take the time to focus on individual tasks. Often quick-tempered, you take orders from few people and live life at a fast pace. Avoid health problems by taking regular time out for rest and relaxation.

Emotionally, it is important that you talk to those you are closest to and work out your true feelings. Once you discover that people are there to help, there is less necessity for you to do everything yourself.

Moon in Taurus

The Moon in Taurus gives you a courteous and friendly manner, which means you are likely to have many friends.

The good things in life mean a lot to you, as Taurus is an Earth sign that delights in experiences which please the senses. Hence you are probably a lover of good food and drink, which may in turn mean you need to keep an eye on the bathroom scales, especially as looking good is also important to you.

Emotionally you are fairly stable and you stick by your own standards. Taureans do not respond well to change. Intuition also plays an important part in your life.

Moon in Gemini

You have a warm-hearted character, sympathetic and eager to help others. At times reserved, you can also be articulate and chatty: this is part of the paradox of Gemini, which always brings duplicity to the nature. You are interested in current affairs, have a good intellect, and are good company and likely to have many friends. Most of your friends have a high opinion of you and would be ready to defend you should the need arise. However, this is usually unnecessary, as you are quite capable of defending yourself in any verbal confrontation.

Travel is important to your inquisitive mind and you find intellectual stimulus in mixing with people from different cultures. You also gain much from reading, writing and the arts but you do need plenty of rest and relaxation in order to avoid fatigue.

Moon in Cancer

The Moon in Cancer at the time of birth is a fortunate position as Cancer is the Moon's natural home. This means that the qualities of compassion and understanding given by the Moon are especially enhanced in your nature, and you are friendly and sociable and cope well with emotional pressures. You cherish home and family life, and happily do the domestic tasks. Your surroundings are important to you and you hate squalor and filth. You are likely to have a love of music and poetry.

Your basic character, although at times changeable like the Moon itself, depends on symmetry. You aim to make your surroundings comfortable and harmonious, for yourself and those close to you.

Moon in Leo

The best qualities of the Moon and Leo come together to make you warm-hearted, fair, ambitious and self-confident. With good organisational abilities, you invariably rise to a position of responsibility in your chosen career. This is fortunate as you don't enjoy being an 'also-ran' and would rather be an important part of a small organisation than a menial in a large one.

You should be lucky in love, and happy, provided you put in the effort to make a comfortable home for yourself and those close to you. It is likely that you will have a love of pleasure, sport, music and literature. Life brings you many rewards, most of them as a direct result of your own efforts, although you may be luckier than average and ready to make the best of any situation.

Moon in Virgo

You are endowed with good mental abilities and a keen receptive memory, but you are never ostentatious or pretentious. Naturally quite reserved, you still have many friends. Marital relationships must be discussed carefully and worked at so that they remain harmonious, as personal attachments can be a problem if you do not give them your full attention.

Talented and persevering, you possess artistic qualities and are a good homemaker. Earning your honours through genuine merit, you work long and hard towards your objectives but show little pride in your achievements. Many short journeys will be undertaken in your life.

Moon in Libra

With the Moon in Libra you are naturally popular and make friends easily. People like you, probably more than you realise, you bring fun to a party and are a natural diplomat. For all its good points, Libra is not the most stable of astrological signs and, as a result, your emotions can be a little unstable too. Therefore, although the Moon in Libra is said to be good for love and marriage, your Sun sign and Rising sign will have an important effect on your emotional and loving qualities.

You must remember to relate to others in your decision-making. Co-operation is crucial because Libra represents the 'balance' of life that can only be achieved through harmonious relationships. Conformity is not easy for you because Libra, an Air sign, likes its independence.

Moon in Scorpio

Some people might call you pushy. In fact, all you really want to do is to live life to the full and protect yourself and your family from the pressures of life. Take care to avoid giving the impression of being sarcastic or impulsive and use your energies wisely and constructively.

You have great courage and you invariably achieve your goals by force of personality and sheer effort. You are fond of mystery and are good at predicting the outcome of situations and events. Travel experiences can be beneficial to you.

You may experience problems if you do not take time to examine your motives in a relationship, and also if you allow jealousy, always a feature of Scorpio, to cloud your judgement.

Moon in Sagittarius

The Moon in Sagittarius helps to make you a generous individual with humanitarian qualities and a kind heart. Restlessness may be intrinsic as your mind is seldom still. Perhaps because of this, you have a need for change that could lead you to several major moves during your adult life. You are not afraid to stand your ground when you know your judgement is right, you speak directly and have good intuition.

At work you are quick, efficient and versatile and so you make an ideal employee. You need work to be intellectually demanding and do not enjoy tedious routines.

In relationships, you anger quickly if faced with stupidity or deception, though you are just as quick to forgive and forget. Emotionally, there are times when your heart rules your head.

Moon in Capricorn

The Moon in Capricorn makes you popular and likely to come into the public eye in some way. The watery Moon is not entirely comfortable in the Earth sign of Capricorn and this may lead to some difficulties in the early years of life. An initial lack of creative ability and indecision must be overcome before the true qualities of patience and perseverance inherent in Capricorn can show through.

You have good administrative ability and are a capable worker, and if you are careful you can accumulate wealth. But you must be cautious and take professional advice in partnerships, as you are open to deception. You may be interested in social or welfare work, which suit your organisational skills and sympathy for others.

Moon in Aquarius

The Moon in Aquarius makes you an active and agreeable person with a friendly, easy-going nature. Sympathetic to the needs of others, you flourish in a laid-back atmosphere. You are broad-minded, fair and open to suggestion, although sometimes you have an unconventional quality which others can find hard to understand.

You are interested in the strange and curious, and in old articles and places. You enjoy trips to these places and gain much from them. Political, scientific and educational work interests you and you might choose a career in science or technology.

Money-wise, you make gains through innovation and concentration and Lunar Aquarians often tackle more than one job at a time. In love you are kind and honest.

Moon in Pisces

You have a kind, sympathetic nature, somewhat retiring at times, but you always take account of others' feelings and help when you can.

Personal relationships may be problematic, but as life goes on you can learn from your experiences and develop a better understanding of yourself and the world around you.

You have a fondness for travel, appreciate beauty and harmony and hate disorder and strife. You may be fond of literature and would make a good writer or speaker yourself. You have a creative imagination and may come across as an incurable romantic. You have strong intuition, maybe bordering on a mediumistic quality, which sets you apart from the mass. You may not be rich in cash terms, but your personal gifts are worth more than gold.

LEO IN LOVE

Discover how compatible in love you are with people from the same and other signs of the zodiac. Five stars equals a match made in heaven!

Leo meets Leo

More of a mutual appreciation society than a relationship, this is a promising match. Leo is kind, considerate, lofty, idealistic and brave, all qualities which are mirrored by a Leo partner. Both Lions will be determined in their ambitions, recognise the importance of the family and share a mutual love in all areas of their lives. Furthermore, Leo loves to be loved and so will give and receive it in equal amounts. There won't be many arguments but when there are – watch out! Star rating: *****

Leo meets Virgo

There is a chance for this couple, but it won't be trouble-free. Leo and Virgo view life very differently: Virgo is of a serious nature, struggling to relate to Leo's relentless optimism and cheerfulness, and even finding it annoying. Leo, meanwhile, may find Virgo stodgy, sometimes dark, and uninspiring. The saving grace comes through communication – Leo knows how to make Virgo talk, which is what it needs. If this pair find happiness, though, it may be a case of opposites attract! Star rating: ***

Leo meets Libra

The biggest drawback here is likely to be in the issue of commitment. Leo knows everything about constancy and faithfulness, a lesson which, sadly, Libra needs to learn. Librans are easy-going and diplomatic, qualities which are useful when Leo is on the war-path. This couple should be compatible on a personal level and any problems tend to relate to the different way in which these signs deal with outside factors. With good will and an open mind, it can work out well enough. Star rating: ***

Leo meets Scorpio

Stand back and watch the sparks fly! Scorpio has the deep sensitivity of a Water sign but it is also partially ruled by Fire planet Mars, from which it draws a great power that Leo will find difficult. Leo loves to take charge and really hates to feel psychologically undermined, which is Scorpio's stock-in-trade. Scorpio may find Leo's ideals a little shallow, which will be upsetting to the Lion. Anything is possible, but this possibility is rather slimmer than most. Star rating: **

Leo meets Sagittarius

An excellent match, as Leo and Sagittarius have so much in common. Their general approach to life is very similar, although as they are both Fire signs they can clash impressively! Sagittarius is shallower and more flippant than Leo likes to think of itself, and the Archer will be the one taking emotional chances. Sagittarius has met its match in the Lion's den, as brave Leo won't be outdone by anyone. Financially, they will either be very wealthy or struggling, and family life may be chaotic. Problems, like joys, are handled jointly – and that leads to happiness. Star rating: *****

Leo meets Capricorn

Despite promising appearances, this match often fails to thrive. Capricorn focuses on long-term objectives and, like Leo, is very practical. Both signs are capable of attaining success after a great struggle, which while requiring effort, gives them a mutual goal. But when life is easier, the cracks begin to show. Capricorn can be too serious for Leo, and the couple share few ideals. Leo loves luxury, Capricorn seeks austerity. Leo is warm but Capricorn seems cold and wintry in comparison. Both have many good points, but they don't seem to fire each other off properly. Star rating: **

Leo meets Aquarius

The problem here is that Aquarius doesn't 'think' in the general sense of the word, it 'knows'. Leo, on the other hand, is more practical and relies more on logical reasoning, and consequently it doesn't understand Aquarius very well. Aquarians can also appear slightly frosty in their appreciation of others and this, too, will eventually annoy Leo. This is a good match for a business partnership because Aquarius is astute, while Leo is brave, but personally the prognosis is less promising. Tolerance, understanding and forbearance are all needed to make this work. Star rating: **

Leo meets Pisces

Pisces always needs to understand others, which makes Leo feel warm and loved, while Leo sees, to its delight, that Pisces needs to be protected and taken care of. Pisceans are often lacking in self-confidence, which is something Leo has to spare, and happily it is often infectious. Pisces' inevitable cares are swept away on a tide of Leonine cheerfulness. This couple's home would be cheerful, and full of love which is beneficial to all family members. This is not a meeting of minds, but rather an understanding and appreciation of differences. Star rating: ****

Leo meets Aries

Stand by for action and make sure that the house is sound-proof! Leo is a lofty idealist and there is always likely to be friction when two Fire signs meet. To compensate, there is much mutual admiration, together with a desire to please. Where there are shared incentives, the prognosis is good but it's important not to let little irritations blow up. Both signs want to have their own way and this is a sure cause of trouble. There might not be much patience here, but there is plenty of action. Star rating: *****

Leo meets Taurus

Here we find a generally successful pairing, which frequently leads to an enduring relationship. Taurus needs stimulation which Leo is happy to offer, while Leo responds well to the Bull's sense of order. The essence of the relationship is balance, but it may be achieved with wild swings of the scales on the way, so don't expect a quiet life, though this pair will enjoy a reconciliation after an argument! Material success is probable and, as both like children, a family is likely. Star rating: ***

Leo meets Gemini

There can be problems here, but Gemini is adaptable enough to overcome many of them. Leo is a go-getter and might sometimes rail against Gemini's flighty tendencies, while Gemini's mental disorganisation can undermine Leo's practicality. However, Leo is cheerful and enjoys Gemini's jokey, flippant qualities. At times of personal intimacy, the two signs should be compatible. Leo and Gemini share very high ideals, but Leo will stick at them for longer. Patience is needed on both sides for the relationship to develop. Star rating: ***

Leo meets Cancer

This relationship will usually be directed by dominant Leo more towards its own needs than Cancer's. However, the Crab will willingly play second fiddle to more progressive and bossy types as it is deeply emotional and naturally supportive. Leo is bright, caring, magnanimous and protective and so, as long as it isn't over-assertive, this could be a good match. On the surface, Cancer appears the more conventional of the two, but Leo will discover, to its delight, that underneath it can be unusual and quirky. Star rating: ****

VENUS:
THE PLANET OF LOVE

If you look up at the sky around sunset or sunrise you will often see Venus in close attendance to the Sun. It is arguably one of the most beautiful sights of all and there is little wonder that historically it became associated with the goddess of love. But although Venus does play an important part in the way you view love and in the way others see you romantically, this is only one of the spheres of influence that it enjoys in your overall character.

Venus has a part to play in the more cultured side of your life and has much to do with your appreciation of art, literature, music and general creativity. Even the way you look is responsive to the part of the zodiac that Venus occupied at the start of your life, though this fact is also down to your Sun sign and Ascending sign. If, at the time you were born, Venus occupied one of the more gregarious zodiac signs, you will be more likely to wear your heart on your sleeve, as well as to be more attracted to entertainment, social gatherings and good company. If on the other hand Venus occupied a quiet zodiac sign at the time of your birth, you would tend to be more retiring and less willing to shine in public situations.

It's good to know what part the planet Venus plays in your life for it can have a great bearing on the way you appear to the rest of the world and since we all have to mix with others, you can learn to make the very best of what Venus has to offer you.

One of the great complications in the past has always been trying to establish exactly what zodiac position Venus enjoyed when you were born because the planet is notoriously difficult to track. However, we have solved that problem by creating a table that is exclusive to your Sun sign, which you will find on the following page.

Establishing your Venus sign could not be easier. Just look up the year of your birth on the following page and you will see a sign of the zodiac. This was the sign that Venus occupied in the period covered by your sign in that year. If Venus occupied more than one sign during the period, this is indicated by the date on which the sign changed, and the name of the new sign. For instance, if you were born in 1970, Venus was in Virgo until the 8th August, after which time it was in Libra. If you were born before 8th August your Venus sign is Virgo, if you were born on or after 8th August, your Venus sign is Libra. Once you have established the position of Venus at the time of your birth, you can then look in the pages which follow to see how this has a bearing on your life as a whole.

1918 LEO / 25.7 VIRGO /
  19.8 LIBRA
1919 VIRGO
1920 LEO / 12.8 VIRGO
1921 GEMINI / 6.8 CANCER
1922 VIRGO / 11.8 LIBRA
1923 CANCER / 4.8 LEO
1924 GEMINI / 25.7 CANCER
1925 LEO / 28.7 VIRGO
1926 LEO / 24.7 VIRGO /
  18.8 VIRGO
1927 VIRGO
1928 LEO / 12.8 VIRGO
1929 GEMINI / 5.8 CANCER
1930 VIRGO / 10.8 LIBRA
1931 CANCER / 3.8 LEO
1932 GEMINI / 28.7 CANCER
1933 LEO / 27.7 VIRGO
1934 LEO / 23.7 VIRGO /
  17.8 LIBRA
1935 VIRGO
1936 LEO / 11.8 VIRGO
1937 GEMINI / 5.8 CANCER
1938 VIRGO / 10.8 LIBRA
1939 CANCER / 3.8 LEO
1940 GEMINI / 1.8 CANCER
1941 LEO / 27.7 VIRGO
1942 LEO / 23.7 VIRGO /
  17.8 LIBRA
1943 VIRGO
1944 LEO / 11.8 VIRGO
1945 GEMINI / 5.8 CANCER
1946 VIRGO / 9.8 LIBRA
1947 CANCER / 2.8 LEO
1948 GEMINI / 3.8 CANCER
1949 LEO / 26.7 VIRGO
1950 LEO / 23.7 VIRGO /
  16.8 LIBRA
1951 VIRGO
1952 LEO / 10.8 VIRGO
1953 GEMINI / 4.8 CANCER
1954 VIRGO / 9.8 LIBRA
1955 CANCER / 1.8 LEO
1956 GEMINI / 4.8 CANCER
1957 LEO / 26.7 VIRGO
1958 VIRGO / 16.8 LIBRA
1959 VIRGO
1960 LEO / 9.8 VIRGO
1961 GEMINI / 4.8 CANCER
1962 VIRGO / 9.8 LIBRA
1963 CANCER / 1.8 LEO
1964 GEMINI / 5.8 CANCER
1965 LEO / 25.7 VIRGO
1966 VIRGO / 16.8 LIBRA

1967 VIRGO
1968 LEO / 9.8 VIRGO
1969 GEMINI / 4.8 CANCER
1970 VIRGO / 8.8 LIBRA
1971 CANCER / 31.7 LEO
1972 GEMINI / 5.8 CANCER
1973 LEO / 25.7 VIRGO
1974 VIRGO / 15.8 LIBRA
1975 VIRGO
1976 LEO / 9.8 VIRGO
1977 GEMINI / 3.8 CANCER
1978 VIRGO / 8.8 LIBRA
1979 CANCER / 31.7 LEO
1980 GEMINI / 6.8 CANCER
1981 LEO / 24.7 VIRGO
1982 VIRGO / 15.8 LIBRA
1983 VIRGO
1984 LEO / 8.8 VIRGO
1985 GEMINI / 3.8 CANCER
1986 VIRGO / 7.8 LIBRA
1987 CANCER / 30.7 LEO
1988 GEMINI / 6.8 CANCER
1989 LEO / 24.7 VIRGO
1990 VIRGO / 14.8 LIBRA
1991 VIRGO / 22.8 LEO
1992 LEO / 8.8 VIRGO
1993 GEMINI / 2.8 CANCER
1994 VIRGO / 7.8 LIBRA
1995 CANCER / 30.7 LEO
1996 GEMINI / 7.8 CANCER
1997 LEO / 24.7 VIRGO
1998 VIRGO / 14.8 LIBRA
1999 VIRGO / 22.8 LEO
2000 LEO / 8.8 VIRGO
2001 GEMINI / 1.8 CANCER
2002 VIRGO / 8.8 LIBRA
2003 CANCER / 30.7 LEO
2004 GEMINI / 7.8 CANCER
2005 LEO / 24.7 VIRGO
2006 VIRGO / 14.8 LIBRA
2007 VIRGO / 22.8 LEO
2008 LEO / 8.8 VIRGO
2009 GEMINI / 1.8 CANCER
2010 VIRGO / 8.8 LIBRA
2011 CANCER / 30.7 LEO
2012 GEMINI / 7.8 CANCER
2013 LEO / 24.7 VIRGO
2014 VIRGO / 14.8 LIBRA
2015 VIRGO / 22.8 LEO
2016 LEO / 6.8 VIRGO

VENUS THROUGH THE ZODIAC SIGNS

Venus in Aries

Amongst other things, the position of Venus in Aries indicates a fondness for travel, music and all creative pursuits. Your nature tends to be affectionate and you would try not to create confusion or difficulty for others if it could be avoided. Many people with this planetary position have a great love of the theatre, and mental stimulation is of the greatest importance. Early romantic attachments are common with Venus in Aries, so it is very important to establish a genuine sense of romantic continuity. Early marriage is not recommended, especially if it is based on sympathy. You may give your heart a little too readily on occasions.

Venus in Taurus

You are capable of very deep feelings and your emotions tend to last for a very long time. This makes you a trusting partner and lover, whose constancy is second to none. In life you are precise and careful and always try to do things the right way. Although this means an ordered life, which you are comfortable with, it can also lead you to be rather too fussy for your own good. Despite your pleasant nature, you are very fixed in your opinions and quite able to speak your mind. Others are attracted to you and historical astrologers always quoted this position of Venus as being very fortunate in terms of marriage. However, if you find yourself involved in a failed relationship, it could take you a long time to trust again.

Venus in Gemini

As with all associations related to Gemini, you tend to be quite versatile, anxious for change and intelligent in your dealings with the world at large. You may gain money from more than one source but you are equally good at spending it. There is an inference here that you are a good communicator, via either the written or the spoken word, and you love to be in the company of interesting people. Always on the look-out for culture, you may also be very fond of music, and love to indulge the curious and cultured side of your nature. In romance you tend to have more than one relationship and could find yourself associated with someone who has previously been a friend or even a distant relative.

Venus in Cancer

You often stay close to home because you are very fond of family and enjoy many of your most treasured moments when you are with those you love. Being naturally sympathetic, you will always do anything you can to support those around you, even people you hardly know at all. This charitable side of your nature is your most noticeable trait and is one of the reasons why others are naturally so fond of you. Being receptive and in some cases even psychic, you can see through to the soul of most of those with whom you come into contact. You may not commence too many romantic attachments but when you do give your heart, it tends to be unconditionally.

Venus in Leo

It must become quickly obvious to almost anyone you meet that you are kind, sympathetic and yet determined enough to stand up for anyone or anything that is truly important to you. Bright and sunny, you warm the world with your natural enthusiasm and would rarely do anything to hurt those around you, or at least not intentionally. In romance you are ardent and sincere, though some may find your style just a little overpowering. Gains come through your contacts with other people and this could be especially true with regard to romance, for love and money often come hand in hand for those who were born with Venus in Leo. People claim to understand you, though you are more complex than you seem.

Venus in Virgo

Your nature could well be fairly quiet no matter what your Sun sign might be, though this fact often manifests itself as an inner peace and would not prevent you from being basically sociable. Some delays and even the odd disappointment in love cannot be ruled out with this planetary position, though it's a fact that you will usually find the happiness you look for in the end. Catapulting yourself into romantic entanglements that you know to be rather ill-advised is not sensible, and it would be better to wait before you committed yourself exclusively to any one person. It is the essence of your nature to serve the world at large and through doing so it is possible that you will attract money at some stage in your life.

Venus in Libra

Venus is very comfortable in Libra and bestows upon those people who have this planetary position a particular sort of kindness that is easy to recognise. This is a very good position for all sorts of friendships and also for romantic attachments that usually bring much joy into your life. Few individuals with Venus in Libra would avoid marriage and since you are capable of great depths of love, it is likely that you will find a contented personal life. You like to mix with people of integrity and intelligence but don't take kindly to scruffy surroundings or work that means getting your hands too dirty. Careful speculation, good business dealings and money through marriage all seem fairly likely.

Venus in Scorpio

You are quite open and tend to spend money quite freely, even on those occasions when you don't have very much. Although your intentions are always good, there are times when you get yourself in to the odd scrape and this can be particularly true when it comes to romance, which you may come to late or from a rather unexpected direction. Certainly you have the power to be happy and to make others contented on the way, but you find the odd stumbling block on your journey through life and it could seem that you have to work harder than those around you. As a result of this, you gain a much deeper understanding of the true value of personal happiness than many people ever do, and are likely to achieve true contentment in the end.

Venus in Sagittarius

You are lighthearted, cheerful and always able to see the funny side of any situation. These facts enhance your popularity. You should never have to look too far to find romantic interest in your life, though it is just possible that you might be too willing to commit yourself before you are certain that the person in question is right for you. Part of the problem here extends to other areas of life too. The fact is that you like variety in everything and so can tire of situations that fail to offer it. All the same, if you choose wisely and learn to understand your restless side, then great happiness can be yours.

47

Venus in Capricorn

The most notable trait that comes from Venus in this position is that it makes you trustworthy and able to take on all sorts of responsibilities in life. People are instinctively fond of you and love you all the more because you are always ready to help those who are in any form of need. Social and business popularity can be yours and there is a magnetic quality to your nature that is particularly attractive in a romantic sense. Anyone who wants a partner for a lover, a spouse and a good friend too would almost certainly look in your direction. Constancy is the hallmark of your nature and unfaithfulness would go right against the grain. You might sometimes be a little too trusting.

Venus in Aquarius

This location of Venus offers a fondness for travel and a desire to try out something new at every possible opportunity. You are extremely easy to get along with and tend to have many friends from varied backgrounds, classes and inclinations. You like to live a distinct sort of life and gain a great deal from moving about, both in a career sense and with regard to your home. It is not out of the question that you could form a romantic attachment to someone who comes from far away or be attracted to a person of a distinctly artistic and original nature. What you cannot stand is jealousy, for you have friends of both sexes and would want to keep things that way.

Venus in Pisces

The first thing people tend to notice about you is your wonderful, warm smile. Being very charitable by nature you will do anything to help others, even if you don't know them well. Much of your life may be spent sorting out situations for other people, but it is very important to feel that you are living for yourself too. In the main, you remain cheerful, and tend to be quite attractive to other people. Where romantic attachments are concerned, you could be drawn to people who are significantly older or younger than yourself or to someone with a unique career or point of view. It might be best for you to avoid marrying whilst you are still very young.

LEO:
2015 DIARY PAGES

October 2015

1 THURSDAY ☿ *Moon Age Day 18 Moon Sign Taurus*

Prepare to make the most of an intellectual peak at the beginning of October by being in the right place at the best time. Your persuasive talents can be put to the test in a number of different ways: professional, practical and even personal. The fact is that you could sell refrigerators to the Inuit at present.

2 FRIDAY ☿ *Moon Age Day 19 Moon Sign Gemini*

Be prepared for minor tensions, particularly at home. You may decide it is better to spend more time with friends right now, taking the heat off domestic situations. At work you should be active and genuinely taking a role when it proves to be most important to do so.

3 SATURDAY ☿ *Moon Age Day 20 Moon Sign Gemini*

Take advantage of the planetary trends that are highlighting creativity. If you are thinking about making changes in and around your home, it might be a good idea to consult your partner. Other family members also have their part to play and it really is a case of being open to opinion now.

4 SUNDAY ☿ *Moon Age Day 21 Moon Sign Gemini*

You are your own best public relations officer today: frank, fearless and bold, yet at the same time caring and willing to listen. These really are the very best qualities of your zodiac sign and they are available for all to see. As a result you ought to find yourself on the receiving end of a very happy day.

5 MONDAY ☿ *Moon Age Day 22 Moon Sign Cancer*

There is a chance that the information you receive from other people will turn out to be interesting and potentially helpful. For this reason alone it is worth keeping your ears open. Even gossip does not fall beneath your contempt for once, though of course being a Leo subject you certainly won't believe everything you hear.

6 TUESDAY ☿ *Moon Age Day 23 Moon Sign Cancer*

For the first part of the day you will be taking things steadily, but once you get the bit between your teeth, it's onwards and upwards once more. Keep an open mind about the attitudes and opinions of a friend, which may sound radical and even quite bonkers. They may simply be going through a tricky period.

7 WEDNESDAY ☿ *Moon Age Day 24 Moon Sign Leo*

You can think big today and tend to make the world your oyster by the sheer dynamism of your personality. Almost anyone you meet can be good to know and useful to have around in a practical sense. What really sets the day apart is the fact that you should be smiling nearly all the time.

8 THURSDAY ☿ *Moon Age Day 25 Moon Sign Leo*

This would be a superb time for putting new ideas into practice. Don't be held back by negative types. Once you have made up your mind, keep moving in that direction. Your social life should be a breeze and with more and more popularity coming your way there are new people joining the fan club.

9 FRIDAY ☿ *Moon Age Day 26 Moon Sign Virgo*

Don't make life any more difficult than it needs to be by chasing up every detail or insisting on having your say. There are times right now when it would definitely be best to keep quiet, rather than to cause problems for yourself. The end of the working week could easily be marred with disputes, though you can avoid them.

10 SATURDAY ☿ *Moon Age Day 27 Moon Sign Virgo*

With the weekend comes a chance to enlist the help and co-operation of other people. It was inevitable right this early in the October that you would vacillate between listening and acting on impulse, but today finds you very compliant. Saturday ought to offer good social prospects and a chance for new enterprises.

11 SUNDAY ☿ *Moon Age Day 28 Moon Sign Virgo*

New and enlivening experiences are just around the next corner. You may become a little frustrated that they don't turn up immediately, but that's the nature of Leo. If you can stay cool, calm and collected, even when you are provoked, there is a good chance you will overcome any obstacle.

12 MONDAY *Moon Age Day 29 Moon Sign Libra*

The spotlight is on your social life, where there could be plenty of lighthearted and enjoyable moments today. Look out for new people coming into your life. They might not signify too much at the moment, but it is only a matter of time before these same individuals begin to play a much more important part in your plans for the future.

13 TUESDAY *Moon Age Day 0 Moon Sign Libra*

You are well in the groove early in the day, even if a few frustrations come along like little dark clouds to spoil your horizons somewhat later. Life is still quite intense, but there is nothing preventing you from taking a break of some sort. Even a slight change in emphasis would be better than nothing.

14 WEDNESDAY *Moon Age Day 1 Moon Sign Scorpio*

Wednesday brings relief from something that has been nagging at you for a while. Circumstances may force you down slower paths, but a little circumspection won't do you any harm at all. Look ahead towards the weekend and work now towards special social functions that have been planned for a while.

15 THURSDAY　　*Moon Age Day 2　Moon Sign Scorpio*

Relationships tend to be rewarding today, which is why you may decide to drop most responsibilities and practical issues in favour of having fun. There are people around who make you laugh, and who are just as fond of you as you are of them. This is definitely not a day during which you need to complicate anything.

16 FRIDAY　　*Moon Age Day 3　Moon Sign Scorpio*

Your co-operative spirit is strong, so don't be afraid to combine your own powers with those of the people you like the most. If there are any individuals around at present who do not care for you, simply shrug your shoulders and accept the fact that you cannot be universally popular.

17 SATURDAY　　*Moon Age Day 4　Moon Sign Sagittarius*

Be prepared for a loved one to rely heavily on your judgement. This implies a high degree of responsibility, but that is not an issue for the Leo nature. You will give the advice you know to be sensible and can be relied upon to offer good counsel and a great deal of natural empathy.

18 SUNDAY　　*Moon Age Day 5　Moon Sign Sagittarius*

You could be in a position to benefit from some good decision-making where money is concerned. Not everyone is willing to support you, however, and you could have trouble with certain acquaintances. In terms of plain friendship, you will find the people who have been around the longest are the ones you want to rely on.

19 MONDAY　　*Moon Age Day 6　Moon Sign Capricorn*

When it comes to talking to colleagues today, you stand a chance of getting a very sympathetic ear and even offers of practical assistance. There is a chance for people you haven't seen for ages to come back into your life any time now, and they may bring with them some heartening and even amusing news.

20 TUESDAY

Moon Age Day 7 Moon Sign Capricorn

Remain open to new input and don't close your mind to anything just because it sounds odd at first. You need to stretch credibility now and to show those around you how keen you are to get on in life. It appears that someone quite important has been watching you, and they are likely to let you know it before long.

21 WEDNESDAY

Moon Age Day 8 Moon Sign Capricorn

There may be a few unexpected demands being made of you now, and that means having to be rather more flexible than has been the case during the last few days. This is particularly true in the case of relatives or friends who are having problems. If you are missing someone, get in touch by letter or email.

22 THURSDAY

Moon Age Day 9 Moon Sign Aquarius

The 'lunar low' can drag you down somewhat if you allow it, so you may feel the need to indulge yourself in some way today. The secret is not to swim against the tide, but to wait for better opportunities to come along. In the meantime, cosset yourself.

23 FRIDAY

Moon Age Day 10 Moon Sign Aquarius

Even if you managed to get at least half way through the 'lunar low' without realising it, there is little assistance about for your plans today. It would be best to keep a low profile for the moment, allowing other people to take some of the strain and being willing to accept intervention and advice.

24 SATURDAY

Moon Age Day 11 Moon Sign Pisces

The focus today appears to be on personal relationships. With everything to play for in the emotional stakes and the weekend offering a good deal of incentive, you need to show those around you, and particularly your romantic partner, how much they mean to you. Social highlights abound.

25 SUNDAY
Moon Age Day 12 Moon Sign Pisces

It could be that you are putting your point of view across in a way that others would see as being contentious. Be careful that you do not cause offence, even unintentionally. Trying to be tactful all the time won't be easy, but it can pay quite definite dividends, both personally and perhaps even financially.

26 MONDAY
Moon Age Day 13 Moon Sign Aries

Professional issues can be complicated today and need careful handling. However, don't allow them to spill over into your personal and social life, which also demand more of your time at present. Consider the needs of friends today and involve them in your plans, particularly someone who is down in the dumps.

27 TUESDAY
Moon Age Day 14 Moon Sign Aries

Look out for minor conflict with others, particularly in group situations. The fact is that you often want to be top dog. Even when you don't, others think that you belong at the head of things. Resolving such difficulties will take patience and tact – though you will still end up running the show.

28 WEDNESDAY
Moon Age Day 15 Moon Sign Taurus

Financial affairs are favoured today. There could be ways and means to increase your income, but you have to dig hard within your own reserves to put some of them into practice. You won't be tardy when it comes to putting your ideas across, especially when you are in the company of people who already think you well on the way to being a genius.

29 THURSDAY
Moon Age Day 16 Moon Sign Taurus

Certain communication issues can be marred by disagreements, which is a pity at a time when you are getting on famously with almost everyone. Convincing colleagues that your ideas are better than theirs won't be easy, but is necessary all the same. By the evening, you will simply want to have a good time.

30 FRIDAY
Moon Age Day 17 Moon Sign Gemini

There are some issues that seem to be a real chore today, and the sadness is that there is no getting away from them. Better by far to pitch in early and to get such jobs out of the way. Later on, you can begin to have some real fun, doing things that have a constant and lasting appeal.

31 SATURDAY
Moon Age Day 18 Moon Sign Gemini

It is unlikely that your home life could be called boring at present. People demand your time and your advice and there is likely to be lots of coming and going. Things could be somewhat quieter if you have to work, however, and you may feel that a little extra incentive is required before long.

November 2015

1 SUNDAY
Moon Age Day 19 Moon Sign Cancer

A new month, but it's business as usual as far as you are concerned. With plenty to keep you occupied, you look forward positively. What might not appeal to you too much is the approach of winter, but you have the chance to create a warm atmosphere in the next couple of months, no matter what the weather is doing.

2 MONDAY
Moon Age Day 20 Moon Sign Cancer

Your ego is boosted when you are at the forefront of situations, so you won't take kindly to being put at the back of any queue right now. Try to stay calm, even if you feel you are under personal pressure and certainly do not defend yourself when it is obvious to almost everyone that you are not under attack.

3 TUESDAY
Moon Age Day 21 Moon Sign Leo

Press ahead with all major plans and don't allow yourself to be held back when you can see that the going is good. There ought to be plenty to occupy your mind and your body today, with this part of the working week likely to be bringing forth new possibilities of both a professional and a personal nature.

4 WEDNESDAY
Moon Age Day 22 Moon Sign Leo

This would be a good time to put your luck to the test. Although you won't want to put your shirt on the next horse running, there could be gains to be made if you take calculated financial risks. Physically and mentally, most Leo subjects should now be firing on all cylinders.

5 THURSDAY
Moon Age Day 23 Moon Sign Leo

Social and romantic issues ought to prove quite satisfying, probably making for an interesting and even a special sort of period. Personal contentment is present and compared with earlier in the week; you are now less likely to react quickly to issues that are not very important.

6 FRIDAY
Moon Age Day 24 Moon Sign Virgo

Not everything on your agenda can be dealt with as quickly or efficiently as you might wish. This means showing patience and also being willing to allow other people to lend a hand. It might be that you have been holding back specific individuals, simply because you will not relinquish control.

7 SATURDAY
Moon Age Day 25 Moon Sign Virgo

There are influences about now that keep you in touch with people you may not see all that often. Your mind tends to travel back as much as it is pushed forwards, and you have a great deal to think about in professional terms. This may turn out to be quite a busy day, though it is diverse and, in most cases, interesting.

8 SUNDAY
Moon Age Day 26 Moon Sign Libra

This might be quite a demanding day, albeit in a low-key sort of way. You move between situations that demand your full attention and there won't be quite the level of rest and relaxation you might wish. There is a forward push on your part to sweep away cobwebs and to see new possibilities that lie before you.

9 MONDAY
Moon Age Day 27 Moon Sign Libra

Your interests are best served by keeping busy and not slacking in any way. People are clearly watching you and the more effort you put in now, the greater the attention focused on you. If you get the chance to take a break later in the day, the change would do you good. Stick with friends at this time.

10 TUESDAY *Moon Age Day 28 Moon Sign Libra*

Getting out and about socially may be just what you need to keep a smile on your face today. Too much commitment to practical issues could prove boring and you will feel much happier with some variety in your life. Romantic issues might be on your mind later in the day. Confidence is reasonably high.

11 WEDNESDAY *Moon Age Day 29 Moon Sign Scorpio*

This should be a lovely time for all intimate matters. Quite a few planetary indicators are suggesting that love is in the air, together with friendship and a feeling of togetherness. The hard edge of Leo certainly isn't on display at this time and it is likely that certain people will realise what an old softy you really are.

12 THURSDAY *Moon Age Day 0 Moon Sign Scorpio*

Be prepared to find yourself suddenly on an emotional roller-coaster. Trying to come to terms with exactly what others expect of you isn't going to be all that easy. Probably the best way to be in the know is the simplest: ask someone!

13 FRIDAY *Moon Age Day 1 Moon Sign Sagittarius*

Minor disagreements, particularly at home, are really not necessary. Instead of falling out, talk things through calmly and rationally. Friends should be co-operative and anxious to have you with them when the good times roll. Although you might be quite tired today, there is a good chance you will join in.

14 SATURDAY *Moon Age Day 2 Moon Sign Sagittarius*

Minor challenges in domestic issues probably cannot be avoided if you stay around at home too much. It would be very easy to become bored during the first part of this weekend. By tomorrow you are on top form again, but for the moment you could do with getting some genuine variety into your life.

15 SUNDAY *Moon Age Day 3 Moon Sign Sagittarius*

The emphasis is on creativity today. It could be that you are making changes around house and home, or perhaps getting involved in some new hobby or pastime. Don't spend too much time doing practical things today. There's nothing wrong with having some fun, too.

16 MONDAY *Moon Age Day 4 Moon Sign Capricorn*

The value of self-reliance and independence is evident for the sign of the Lion today. All in all, you are in for a fairly positive time. You can't expect everyone to like you, but at least you have it within your nature now to ignore the people who do not. Getting to your chosen objectives ought to be a piece of cake.

17 TUESDAY *Moon Age Day 5 Moon Sign Capricorn*

There are opportunities for pleasurable travel, even though this may not be the best part of the year weather-wise. At any rate, you need a change of scenery. Those Leo people who find it possible to take a winter holiday would certainly enjoy getting away now. Consideration for other people appears to be high.

18 WEDNESDAY *Moon Age Day 6 Moon Sign Aquarius*

There are some limitations to be faced today and tomorrow. This is more or less entirely due to the 'lunar low' and there probably isn't very much you can do about the situation. Instead of bemoaning the fact, enjoy some rest and relaxation. There is no barrier to having fun, especially when this is of a low-key form.

19 THURSDAY *Moon Age Day 7 Moon Sign Aquarius*

There is a warning around today not to take any big risks. Be willing to settle for a peaceful life and allow others to take the strain. You are undergoing sea-changes in thinking at the moment and it is helpful for you to take some moments for reflection. In reality, you should get a good deal more done right now than you expect.

20 FRIDAY
Moon Age Day 8 Moon Sign Pisces

Only you can decide whether or not to believe everything you hear today. Be cautious, however, because at least some of it will be true. Confidence is growing all the time in a professional sense, but you can be too clever for your own good. It is important to check and recheck all facts and figures before proceeding with any specific deal.

21 SATURDAY
Moon Age Day 9 Moon Sign Pisces

Get an early start with all important projects and ideas. The more you get done in the morning, the greater the amount of time you will have to please yourself later. It might be difficult to prevent yourself from doing tasks that rightfully belong in the middle of next week, but that's just the way you are feeling now.

22 SUNDAY
Moon Age Day 10 Moon Sign Aries

The green light is on and you are keen to get on with specific projects. The help you need is surely present, though in the main you are happiest when working alone. Not everyone will have your best interests at heart, though it isn't hard to tell who wants to stab you in the back.

23 MONDAY
Moon Age Day 11 Moon Sign Aries

This is a perfect day to be in the thick of things socially and some of the less than positive associations of yesterday are now dissipating fast. Congratulations may be in order somewhere in your friendship circle and you will want to be the first to offer them. Concentrate when dealing with financial matters.

24 TUESDAY
Moon Age Day 12 Moon Sign Taurus

A more competitive edge shows today, especially when you are involved in discussions of any sort. Confidence is growing to overthrow obstacles that have been around a while, especially at work. You are able to score a genuine coup over someone who hasn't shown much interest in your wellbeing.

25 WEDNESDAY   *Moon Age Day 13 Moon Sign Taurus*

You are popular and attractive at the moment, not that this is anything new for the average Leo. All the same, it shows and you can't avoid realising when someone is giving you the come on. Whether or not you respond depends on your availability, but be careful: this is no time to take emotional chances.

26 THURSDAY   *Moon Age Day 14 Moon Sign Gemini*

There should be no problems with your ego at present. Your popularity remains intact and, once again, it isn't hard for you to notice when people like you. Naturally inclined to speak the truth at the moment, you are drawn into offering the sort of assistance that you would hardly have expected.

27 FRIDAY   *Moon Age Day 15 Moon Sign Gemini*

Your powers of attraction are in the ascendant and you would rarely find a better day for appealing to someone you have fancied for a while. If this merely represents a fantasy, there is probably no harm done. Don't be too quick to judge a friend who has acted rashly.

28 SATURDAY   *Moon Age Day 16 Moon Sign Cancer*

It might be a good idea to keep certain plans on ice, if only for today. Everything you want can be yours, but just not right now. Spend time with your friends and maybe an hour or two on your own, planning for the future. Finances need careful handling and, if possible, hang on to money for the moment.

29 SUNDAY   *Moon Age Day 17 Moon Sign Cancer*

With the Sun now firmly in your solar fourth house, it is fun to be around people you know and like. Although just as sociable as ever, there is still that small matter of trust, which has been bugging you for a few days. When you are with those you have known for years, this won't be a problem.

30 MONDAY   *Moon Age Day 18 Moon Sign Cancer*

If a mini-crisis turns up on the domestic scene, stop everything and sort it out immediately. In the main, it is the social aspects of life that you still enjoy the most and you probably will not find yourself tied too much to professional considerations. Find a few moments simply to sit and contemplate life.

♌ December

2015

1 TUESDAY
Moon Age Day 19 Moon Sign Leo

You could do worse than to stay close to those around you who have real power, particularly at work. Your own ideas are sound, and worth discussing with anyone who is willing to listen. Once work is out of the way, you show a great capacity for simply having a good time.

2 WEDNESDAY
Moon Age Day 20 Moon Sign Leo

This is the best part of the month when it comes to having the necessary get up and go to really change your life and its circumstances. With a good deal of empathy, and a great desire to please others, there is no reason at all why you should ruffle any feathers. Life is hectic, but it should be settled too.

3 THURSDAY
Moon Age Day 21 Moon Sign Virgo

You are aware that give and take is important today and you are unlikely to lose sight of that fact. You might have to be a bit devious if you want to get your own way and yet still let others know how committed you are to them. Don't tell any lies, even if you have to be somewhat liberal with the truth.

4 FRIDAY
Moon Age Day 22 Moon Sign Virgo

Although you could find there are one or two professional setbacks to be addressed, in the main you are still progressive, hopeful and aspirational. Turn your mind away from work later in the day, towards fun and games, which become an increasing part of your life as the month advances. Confidence remains solid.

5 SATURDAY · *Moon Age Day 23 Moon Sign Libra*

This is a time to be seeking wide, open spaces. The weekend offers a sense of freedom and the chance to do something different. What you wouldn't take kindly to right now is being restricted in any way. There are plenty of people around you who would be only too pleased to join you on a flight of fancy.

6 SUNDAY · *Moon Age Day 24 Moon Sign Libra*

There are others to contend with today, one or two of whom are anxious for you to follow their lead. To do so probably won't appeal and the difficulty lies in letting them know this fact, without inadvertently offering offence. A little mistake made early in the day should be easy to put right later.

7 MONDAY · *Moon Age Day 25 Moon Sign Libra*

This is a day on which you should have plenty to say for yourself and no shortage of energy with which to get things done. Creature comforts are not all that important to you at the moment and you are quite prepared to go through some discomfort in order to achieve your objectives. You are also extremely friendly today.

8 TUESDAY · *Moon Age Day 26 Moon Sign Scorpio*

Your best area at the moment comes through travel, mental exercise of almost any sort and simple human contact. Still friendly, and very anxious to help, you seek out good causes right now and do whatever you can to get the rest of the world into the same pre-Christmas spirit that you presently experience.

9 WEDNESDAY · *Moon Age Day 27 Moon Sign Scorpio*

Your interests are best served by going with the flow today. There are gains to be made in a number of different directions and as you already have your social head on, the run-up to Christmas probably begins here for you. Concentrate on specific tasks that could prove awkward if you lose sight of the major objectives.

10 THURSDAY *Moon Age Day 28 Moon Sign Sagittarius*

Look out for small pressures coming from a number of different directions. Calm down an overactive nervous system and avoid allowing yourself to be become too fixated about any aspect of life. Cool and steady is what works for you best this Thursday, and you are more than capable of adopting this state.

11 FRIDAY *Moon Age Day 0 Moon Sign Sagittarius*

This could be one of the best days of the month for a new start at work. Of course, you might find this difficult with Christmas just around the corner, but you can start a few balls rolling and will probably be pleased to do so. Co-operation with co-workers can also be a key to success.

12 SATURDAY *Moon Age Day 1 Moon Sign Sagittarius*

Since work matters seem to be fairly progressive and, in the main, looking after themselves, you will probably be turning your attention to other matters. Confidence remains generally high on the social scene, and you may decide to embark upon new interests that have been at the back of your mind for a while.

13 SUNDAY *Moon Age Day 2 Moon Sign Capricorn*

A loved one, perhaps your romantic partner, will probably be expressing some rather strong opinions at present. Be creative in your responses and don't allow yourself to become unsettled by matters that you can deal with quite easily. There are some interesting opportunities to change aspects of your personal life.

14 MONDAY *Moon Age Day 3 Moon Sign Capricorn*

Don't be afraid to stand out in a crowd, because your ego requires boosting as much as possible. Avoid family arguments, which cannot help you in any way at the moment, and try to take a generally optimistic view of life. Give yourself chance to relax, once the daily grind is over.

15 TUESDAY
Moon Age Day 4 Moon Sign Aquarius

There is much to be said for avoiding too much work today. The 'lunar low' makes you lethargic and much more willing than usual to put your feet up. Keep a low profile socially, too, maybe settling for spending some hours on your own. The rest should do you good.

16 WEDNESDAY
Moon Age Day 5 Moon Sign Aquarius

This may be another reasonably quiet day. For those Leo subjects who already have their Christmas heads on, this might be a good period to look ahead and to plan. This ought to be a slightly better day on the social front and romance is around for those of you who want to make yourselves available to greet it.

17 THURSDAY
Moon Age Day 6 Moon Sign Pisces

Doing your own thing seems to be the key to happiness at the moment, though maybe you have things slightly wrong. Join in some family fun and you will lighten the professional load you could be carrying at present. There is a need to bolster the resolve of a friend who is trying to alter his or her life. Only you can help with this.

18 FRIDAY
Moon Age Day 7 Moon Sign Pisces

Although your sense of professional commitment is reasonably good, you should be turning your attention towards the practical necessities of life today. Getting ready for Christmas is one thing that you address and you may also be busy working out how to improve general family resources in the weeks ahead.

19 SATURDAY
Moon Age Day 8 Moon Sign Aries

High spirits prevail, and the sense of joy that is so important to your zodiac sign is well in evidence. Not everyone is quite as happy as you are today, though you do have the capacity to cheer up others if you put your mind to the task. Personal issues demand a matter of fact attitude at present.

20 SUNDAY   *Moon Age Day 9 Moon Sign Aries*

There are a number of obligations around today that leave little time for you to concentrate on your own life. Since this is fairly typical of the sort of person you are, it probably will not worry you too much, if at all. Last-minute planning for Christmas is part of the recipe for an interesting Sunday.

21 MONDAY   *Moon Age Day 10 Moon Sign Aries*

Avoid being too extravagant today. There is a possibility that you are spending money you don't actually possess, and this could lead to a few worries towards the very end of the year or in January. You need to be realistic, and to persuade those around you to take a similar attitude.

22 TUESDAY   *Moon Age Day 11 Moon Sign Taurus*

What matters most today is feeling useful and being able to offer sound advice to people who have problems of one sort or another. You are entering a very positive phase romantically speaking, and one that predominates until well after Christmas. Not everyone is being equally co-operative, however.

23 WEDNESDAY   *Moon Age Day 12 Moon Sign Taurus*

Practical matters are likely to turn out the way you would wish. Last-minute planning and preparations should go well, but you could be slightly bothered by the attitude of friends, which seems odd. Family members will be pestering you all the time, especially younger people, but this probably won't be a problem to you.

24 THURSDAY   *Moon Age Day 13 Moon Sign Gemini*

Prepare to make the most of a brand-new influence that increases your desire for new experiences and causes you to throw over traditions and routines willingly. This is fine for you, but with Christmas only just around the corner, you have to respect the fact that some people close to you want to leave things the way they are.

25 FRIDAY
Moon Age Day 14 Moon Sign Gemini

There is something distinctly weird and wonderful about Christmas Day, though not in a difficult sense. Out-of-the-ordinary experiences are likely, together with messages from people you may not have been in contact with for ages. All in all, this is a day for good communications and for enjoying the antics of others.

26 SATURDAY
Moon Age Day 15 Moon Sign Cancer

Boxing Day will find you busy and very progressive in attitude. However, the important aspects of today could easily be romantic ones. Maybe it's the time of year or perhaps your own attitude, but you should find that your partner is very much more responsive and inclined to say just the right things to you.

27 SUNDAY
Moon Age Day 16 Moon Sign Cancer

It is clear that you want to remain busy and useful at this time, though you fall short of the total energy that is coming your way tomorrow. It is no sin to take a rest and after all that is part of what holidays are about. Don't shy away from a discussion that you know to be absolutely necessary.

28 MONDAY
Moon Age Day 17 Moon Sign Leo

The 'lunar high' arrives today, adding extra oomph to your life and putting you in a party mood that might not have been totally present so far this Christmas. It takes people with real energy to keep up with you and you tend to mix best with those who hold similar values to your own.

29 TUESDAY
Moon Age Day 18 Moon Sign Leo

You can learn something new and exciting now. Keep your ears open and be willing to alter your plans at the last minute in order to achieve something splendid. The period between Christmas and New Year is turning out to be a hectic one, but don't forget that part of the reason for holidays is to have a rest.

30 WEDNESDAY   *Moon Age Day 19 Moon Sign Virgo*

You can afford to say exactly what you feel, and yet make everyone around you feel very special indeed. Surprises are in store, which isn't all that odd at this time, though some of them will far surpass your expectations.

31 THURSDAY   *Moon Age Day 20 Moon Sign Virgo*

Your social life ought to prove quite rewarding. Creative potential is good and you may have decided to make some sort of change at home. As long as it is something that makes you more comfortable and not less, then your efforts are worthwhile. Let someone else undertake a domestic task.

LEO:
2016 DIARY PAGES

LEO:
YOUR YEAR IN BRIEF

This is the sort of year that Leo should relish. Do not be disheartened if things are not working out as you would wish as the year begins, this won't matter too much in the longer term. Many of the gains you make this year come as a result of your desire to break new ground and to show how capable you are. January and February are amongst the best times to make significant changes and there should be plenty of help around if you feel you need it.

March and April bring their own small problems but in the end you should discover that, with patience and perseverance, you can overcome obstacles and push through to your chosen destination. March, especially, is good for romance, whilst April is more materialistic in nature and much depends on your own ingenuity – which happily is right on the ball throughout most of the month.

With the arrival of the early summer, May and June should bring the most positive trends of the year so far. You have the necessary determination to make headway in your life. Romance looks good through the warmer months and there should be plenty of opportunity to travel. Don't get too tied down with domestic details. Any problems at this time could be related to the fact that you are doing more than is strictly good for you at times.

As July arrives you will be keen to get out and about and won't take kindly to being restricted in any way in your movements. Both July and August offer opportunities that come as a result of travel and you will also be keen to make alterations of some sort to your living space. Both months are about activity and you will be busy socially – perhaps in some ways much more so than you may have expected. Love is also likely to come knocking at this time.

Along comes the autumn and during September and October you will be looking to see what you can do to feather your own nest in a financial sense. You need security and will be unhappy if you feel that things are not as solid as you might wish. You should still be very keen to do what you can to inspire new social contacts and you may also have good cause to be proud of family members.

The last two months of the year, November and December, will find you slightly quieter but equally determined to get what you want from life. There are gains to be made in a practical and a financial sense and you seem to be everywhere at the same time. Being busy isn't a problem to you but it could mean you are late this year with your Christmas arrangements. Expect a happy family time and a positive end to the year.

♌ *January* 2016

1 FRIDAY
Moon Age Day 21   Moon Sign Virgo

Stand by for a positive start to the year but be prepared to vary your routines in order to get the very best from the day. It may be necessary to do some fairly routine jobs while still having fun. When it comes to confronting people who have unnerved you in the past it would be sensible to remain bold.

2 SATURDAY
Moon Age Day 22   Moon Sign Libra

Trends suggest this will be a good weekend socially. Not everyone falls in line with your plans but it should be possible to talk others round to what seems a sensible point of view when looked at from your side. Money matters could be variable but will soon be on the up. Definitely a day to seek out some fun.

3 SUNDAY
Moon Age Day 23   Moon Sign Libra

Gathering resources is likely to be number one on your list of priorities today. This is potentially a very practical period and one that allows for growth in several areas of your life. In particular you should notice that relationships are working well and possibly offering a number of unexpected opportunities.

4 MONDAY
Moon Age Day 24   Moon Sign Scorpio

Peace and quiet might be difficult to find at the start of this new working week. The trouble is that you seem to have so much to do you may have to spread yourself too thinly for your own peace of mind. Make sure that at least part of the day is given over to having fun and simply pleasing yourself.

5 TUESDAY   *Moon Age Day 25   Moon Sign Scorpio*

Keep your options open when it comes to making big decisions. The more you are willing to look at the wider picture, the greater is the likelihood that you will get what you are looking for. The attitude of loved ones can be hard to fathom at this time, though less so if you put yourself in their shoes.

6 WEDNESDAY   ☿ *Moon Age Day 26   Moon Sign Scorpio*

Although your domestic life could prove to be somewhat demanding at this time, you may find that you can move forward on other fronts. Beware of a tendency to dwell on matters that are really not important and be prepared to attend to jobs that have been waiting around for some time. Friends should prove supportive.

7 THURSDAY   ☿ *Moon Age Day 27   Moon Sign Sagittarius*

There is little reason now why plans of almost any sort should fail to proceed in an orderly and disciplined manner. Of course you can't rely on the support of everyone you know, but the people who won't play ball may not be too important. The boring but unavoidable jobs for the day should be undertaken early.

8 FRIDAY   ☿ *Moon Age Day 28   Moon Sign Sagittarius*

Casual contacts appear to work well for you at present and should continue to do so for the remainder of the month at least. This is not a Friday for taking yourself or anyone else too seriously. Be bold when necessary, even if there are times when it is more sensible to simply go with the flow.

9 SATURDAY   ☿ *Moon Age Day 0   Moon Sign Capricorn*

Whilst the social scene is potentially exciting this weekend, there is still the feeling that some matters are not working out quite as you would wish at home. Just as well then that you tend to be out and about for much of the time. Arguments won't help at the moment and don't forget appointments or birthdays.

10 SUNDAY ☿ *Moon Age Day 1   Moon Sign Capricorn*

The going should be good when practical matters demand your attention. Family members will be demanding more of you than usual and it is important not to forget certain responsibilities that may have fallen by the wayside of late. Don't be afraid to ask for something you really want.

11 MONDAY ☿ *Moon Age Day 2   Moon Sign Aquarius*

It is best to conserve your efforts at the moment. This is the time of the monthly 'lunar low' and that will make it difficult for you to make real progress. As long as you realise this fact and don't spend today or tomorrow knocking your head against a brick wall, the period can be fruitful and even enjoyable.

12 TUESDAY ☿ *Moon Age Day 3   Moon Sign Aquarius*

Strangely enough, despite the presence of the 'lunar low', this can be a very lucky time. Good fortune may come along at unexpected moments and it is sensible to make the most of opportunities as and when they present themselves. Avoid disagreements with people who could prove to be very important to you later on.

13 WEDNESDAY ☿ *Moon Age Day 4   Moon Sign Pisces*

The ability to have supreme confidence in your ideas isn't always forthcoming, even for a Leo. All the same it proves essential right now. Some leeway may be necessary when looking at the ideas and opinions of others, particularly those of younger family members. Practically speaking this is an enterprising and interesting period.

14 THURSDAY ☿ *Moon Age Day 5   Moon Sign Pisces*

Career-wise you are likely to be firing on all cylinders and could find yourself in the midst of one of the most entertaining days of the month. Routines are better left for another time now and instead leave some space to simply have fun. Avoid discussions with people you know to be unreasonable if you can.

15 FRIDAY ☿ *Moon Age Day 6   Moon Sign Pisces*

It is possible that a personal issue may be hard to resolve at this time. Don't worry if this happens as you can deal with it later. For now you are very busy with practical matters and also with getting on professionally. Although social instincts are also very strong at this time, moments to spare are few and far between.

16 SATURDAY ☿ *Moon Age Day 7   Moon Sign Aries*

It is to be hoped that you will make the best of a rather involved, fast-moving sort of weekend. It would be sensible to allow your mind to wander. You are in need of something that will bring a breath of fresh air into your life. Even a slight alteration to your winter routine would be of great help at present.

17 SUNDAY ☿ *Moon Age Day 8   Moon Sign Aries*

A period of emotional ups and downs can be expected now. Working out exactly why people are behaving in the way they are can take up some of your time, but in a general sense specific individuals will prove to be something of a mystery. Try to find a little social enjoyment when the working day is over.

18 MONDAY ☿ *Moon Age Day 9   Moon Sign Taurus*

Egos can get in the way at the start of this week, especially at work. It would be wise to make certain that one of those egos is not yours. Allow other people their own opinions and don't dominate – as Leo people sometimes do. The more open you are today, the better will be the response coming from others.

19 TUESDAY ☿ *Moon Age Day 10   Moon Sign Taurus*

A family issue is likely to bring you down to earth with a bump at this stage of the working week. Of course this matter will have to be dealt with but you should not allow it to divert you from practical progress, something that is also on your mind at the moment. Listen to the sound advice of a good friend.

20 WEDNESDAY ☿ *Moon Age Day 11   Moon Sign Gemini*

Social matters may be preferable to domestic affairs, at least for now. There may, however, be certain domestic tasks that you cannot put off any longer and it's important to realise that balance is necessary in your life at the moment. Stick to a few trusted routines and all should be well in the end.

21 THURSDAY ☿ *Moon Age Day 12   Moon Sign Gemini*

Don't expect your views to go unchallenged at home. If the people who are pulling you up in your tracks are not the sort of individuals to cross you as a rule, consider that perhaps they have a valid point. It is very important to see the other person's point of view right now and to let them know that you are doing so.

22 FRIDAY ☿ *Moon Age Day 13   Moon Sign Cancer*

A new trend emerges which may help you to see a simpler way to manage your home life. Armed with this knowledge, you have plenty of enthusiasm for all practical matters and an ability to move progressively towards your most important objectives. Some travel could prove both necessary and interesting now.

23 SATURDAY ☿ *Moon Age Day 14   Moon Sign Cancer*

For weekend-working Leos this can prove to be an important day. Not that you should worry if you are away from your professional surroundings. There are gains to be made in any case, though generally speaking in practical matters. A good day for shopping or for hunting out a bargain in a more unusual way.

24 SUNDAY ☿ *Moon Age Day 15   Moon Sign Leo*

It is likely that you will find yourself somewhat better off now than you might have expected. If this turns out to be the case, use the extra cash wisely and don't allow yourself to be held back by the negative ideas and opinions of others. You may also find the time to deal with tasks that have been waiting in the wings for a while.

25 MONDAY ☿ *Moon Age Day 16   Moon Sign Leo*

The 'lunar high' brings the first genuine breath of fresh air into your life that you have noticed since the start of the year. Put all your energy to work in terms of feathering your own nest, and that of family members. Avoid being bogged down by details at this time because it is the future that matters now.

26 TUESDAY ☿ *Moon Age Day 17   Moon Sign Leo*

This ought to be another rewarding day. There are many things on your mind, yet you are not intimidated by the thought of all that has to be done. When it comes to deciding how you should proceed, intuition can be an excellent guide at present. In amongst the hustle and bustle of life a sort of calmness should descend.

27 WEDNESDAY *Moon Age Day 18   Moon Sign Virgo*

It may be that there are elements of your domestic life that require special attention right now. Arguments within the family should not be allowed to spoil this part of the week, and particularly so if they have nothing to do with you. It is possible for you to play the part of the honest broker at some stage.

28 THURSDAY *Moon Age Day 19   Moon Sign Virgo*

You seem to be especially pushy at the moment and this could be said to be the first time this year when the most progressive qualities of your zodiac sign are showing themselves fully. Make the most of these trends and do what you can to ensure that everyone knows that you are about and active.

29 FRIDAY *Moon Age Day 20   Moon Sign Libra*

A sure-footed action at work appears to put you firmly in the driving seat. It may appear that others are getting the better of you, though this is unlikely to actually be the case. As long as you monitor your actions and know that you are working from a base of sensible motives, things should turn out to your advantage.

30 SATURDAY   *Moon Age Day 21   Moon Sign Libra*

A period of social harmony emerges and offers you the chance to come to terms with a wayward family member, or a series of people who have been causing slight problems in your life in the recent past. There's a long way to go in practical issues but a few important journeys are underway.

31 SUNDAY   *Moon Age Day 22   Moon Sign Libra*

The very end of this month is the best time for employing new strategies and for taking the initiative. This might not seem particularly easy to achieve on a Sunday but you may be surprised at just how much headway you are able to make. Find a way to spoil yourself a little later in the day.

February 2016

1 MONDAY
Moon Age Day 23   Moon Sign Scorpio

Today should bring a breath of fresh air. Get all necessary jobs out of the way early and then save some time to simply enjoy yourself. The positions of several of the planets in your chart is likely to bring stability to your relationships and help you to display the most attractive side of your nature to the world.

2 TUESDAY
Moon Age Day 24   Moon Sign Scorpio

It appears that you can get the best from others in terms of communication today. This part of the working week is likely to find you anxious to get on practically. Accept that not everything can be sorted out at the same time and that a little patience may be called for. Not the most natural trait for a Leo!

3 WEDNESDAY
Moon Age Day 25   Moon Sign Sagittarius

The area of life that genuinely responds to your own efforts at the moment is friendship. There are all sorts of people around right now who are simply bursting to do you a favour. Try not to get too excited regarding plans that might have to be substantially altered further down the line.

4 THURSDAY
Moon Age Day 26   Moon Sign Sagittarius

Warm and intimate attachments bring the best moments now. Already planning for the weekend you are nevertheless likely to be happy to stay at home and put your feet up by a warm fire. This is also an ideal day to look ahead and to plan some fairly long journeys that you may wish to take later.

5 FRIDAY
Moon Age Day 27   Moon Sign Sagittarius

You probably won't be in the market for advice today. Leo can be quite headstrong, though it would be sensible to bite your lip rather than to fall out with someone who genuinely does have your best interests at heart. What might bug you the most right now is the realisation that you can't avoid certain rules and regulations.

6 SATURDAY
Moon Age Day 28   Moon Sign Capricorn

Today should be good for considering professional matters, even if the arrival of the weekend prevents you from actually doing anything about them. Meanwhile the social trends look reasonably good, and particularly so if you are in the company of people who simply want to have a joyful time.

7 SUNDAY
Moon Age Day 29   Moon Sign Capricorn

In almost every way you can find yourself on a winning streak today. The week ahead particularly good and you should have plenty of reason to be cheerful. If this isn't easy with the cold of winter hanging around, take yourself to a place that is warm and meet some people who make you laugh.

8 MONDAY
Moon Age Day 0   Moon Sign Aquarius

Setbacks are a real possibility but should not be taken too seriously. Look at the game plan of life as a whole and you should be quite pleased with the progress you are making. Excitement isn't easy to find at present but you will find yourself in the company of people who have genuinely diverting ways.

9 TUESDAY
Moon Age Day 1   Moon Sign Aquarius

If anyone is trying to manipulate you, or force you down paths that you don't wish to follow, you are very unlikely to play ball at the moment. The more stubborn side of your zodiac sign appears to be on display at present, causing you to dig your heels in. Social trends look good, particularly in the evening.

10 WEDNESDAY *Moon Age Day 2   Moon Sign Pisces*

The things that happen in your personal life can make you smile today. This is an area of life that may not have captivated you very much of late. Maybe this would be a good moment to buy a small gift for your lover, or to simply take the time to say 'thank you' for a gesture that has been made recently.

11 THURSDAY *Moon Age Day 3   Moon Sign Pisces*

Certain aspects of life could prove to be rather unreliable. What really matters is listening to information that comes your way carefully and then sifting through it for the truth. You may be troubled by the perceived unreliability of others but the truth may be that you are looking for a degree of commitment that simply does not exist.

12 FRIDAY *Moon Age Day 4   Moon Sign Aries*

Entertainment brings out the best in you, whether you are creating it for others or enjoying something that comes in from outside. Gregarious and fun to have around you should have very little difficulty finding friends at present and show an extremely happy face to the world at large.

13 SATURDAY *Moon Age Day 5   Moon Sign Aries*

Your ability to make effective changes might seem to be somewhat limited, which is why it would be better to spend the weekend doing what takes your fancy. Mix and mingle with those who are of a fairly easy-going nature and learn from them how important it is to believe that everything can turn out fine.

14 SUNDAY *Moon Age Day 6   Moon Sign Taurus*

Although it is still quite early in the year, trends show that all outdoor pursuits suit you at present. That might be somewhat strange because Leo, definitely a summer zodiac sign, usually prefers to stay in the warm. Perhaps it is the intrepid side of your Fire-sign nature that forces you out into the February air.

15 MONDAY — *Moon Age Day 7   Moon Sign Taurus*

Leisure and entertainment continue to be right up your street today. Not everyone shares your enthusiasm for having a good time so do be careful how much pressure you put on those around you when it comes to joining in. Refuse to be bullied by anyone today – even valued and loved family members.

16 TUESDAY — *Moon Age Day 8   Moon Sign Gemini*

Today you can expect another day of generally smooth progress. This stage of the working week ought to find you more than willing to join forces with others in order to get ahead. Some of these individuals may be very strange bedfellows but if you have the right attitude at present, you can ally yourself with almost anyone.

17 WEDNESDAY — *Moon Age Day 9   Moon Sign Gemini*

Practical matters may turn out to be especially rewarding today. Push on towards success in your professional life, and then give your time readily for the greater good once work is out of the way. You may find some time at the end of the day to simply enjoy yourself, although perhaps not a great deal.

18 THURSDAY — *Moon Age Day 10   Moon Sign Cancer*

Trends suggest that this could be the best time to make new social contacts ahead of the weekend. Routines can be dealt with very easily indeed and you may become more aware than usual of the cyclical nature of life. Don't be surprised if quite a few coincidences seem to occur. These could act as messengers.

19 FRIDAY — *Moon Age Day 11   Moon Sign Cancer*

The things you hear today may put you firmly in the picture when it comes to general life improvements. The daily grind won't interest you in the slightest and it is clear that you want to do the exciting jobs, leaving the rest to others. Those Leo individuals who are looking for romance could have the advantage.

20 SATURDAY   *Moon Age Day 12   Moon Sign Cancer*

The planets indicate that a new period of regeneration begins in your life today. For the next three or four weeks you can expect to make quite a few changes, the vast majority of which work to your advantage. Cutting out the dead wood from your professional and practical sphere of influence is a process that can start immediately.

21 SUNDAY   *Moon Age Day 13   Moon Sign Leo*

With the Moon back in your zodiac sign there is everything to play for today. This is not a period when you are likely to be hanging in the background. On the contrary it is very likely that what you say is being noted in high places. The present trends also look good from the point of view of romance.

22 MONDAY   *Moon Age Day 14   Moon Sign Leo*

The planetary peak is still in place, even if the way it impacts on your life today is more personal than practical. Getting on with others should be easy enough, as will making space for new ventures. In particular, an idea that has been at the back of your mind for a while can be exploited fully now.

23 TUESDAY   *Moon Age Day 15   Moon Sign Virgo*

It is possible that you will be more reluctant to get involved in social events today than would normally be the case. You probably feel the urge to spend time on your own, or at least in the company of people you see as being very close to you. Not a bad period for finding a warm fire and toasting your toes.

24 WEDNESDAY   *Moon Age Day 16   Moon Sign Virgo*

Don't expect everything to go according to plan today. If you do, there are disappointments on the way. If, on the other hand, you accept a good deal of what life is putting in your path, you can respond positively to prevailing trends. Love is one of the areas of life that should please you greatly at this time.

25 THURSDAY   *Moon Age Day 17   Moon Sign Libra*

You can expect a more productive period at work now. Getting to grips with issues that have bugged you for some time seems to be a piece of cake under today's trends. Meanwhile you find new friendships coming your way, together with a change in the emphasis of established relationships. Home and work are of equal importance at present.

26 FRIDAY   *Moon Age Day 18   Moon Sign Libra*

Avoid any tendency to believe that the grass is greener on the other side of the fence. What you have and the way you deal with it should be enough for this Friday, since you are not exactly firing on all cylinders for a few hours. Progress may be made later in the day, probably as a result of loving attachments.

27 SATURDAY   *Moon Age Day 19   Moon Sign Libra*

A loved one is likely to require fairly sensitive handling at present. Finding the time to treat people in the way you know to be correct shouldn't be difficult right now, because Saturday offers a few hours to reflect. A change of scene would do you good, so listen to the suggestions that are being made.

28 SUNDAY   *Moon Age Day 20   Moon Sign Scorpio*

Material progress is not only possible but very likely today. As a result this is unlikely to be a lazy, stay-at-home sort of Sunday. On the contrary you are seeking out bargains, talking to the right people and generally doing what it takes to feather your nest. Weekend-working Leo individuals fare the best of all today.

29 MONDAY   *Moon Age Day 21   Moon Sign Scorpio*

You won't be backward at coming forward in terms of encouraging others to do your bidding at any time this week, but especially today. Racing into a brand new Monday you appear gregarious, very friendly but urgent in your desire to succeed. More haste and less speed might be the adage for you at present.

March

2016

1 TUESDAY
Moon Age Day 22   Moon Sign Sagittarius

This is an ideal day to persuade others on to the same mental wavelength as you. With good powers of communication and a willingness to take on board the other person's point of view, a great deal could be achieved. There could be small gains arising as a result of past efforts and the way you view them now.

2 WEDNESDAY
Moon Age Day 23   Moon Sign Sagittarius

Today you may experience a little confusion over a personal matter. If this is the case all you can do is seek out some advice or to wait until matters sort themselves out. What you won't be keen to do is to allow your recent progress to be slowed. Coming to terms with the past should at least be easier now.

3 THURSDAY
Moon Age Day 24   Moon Sign Sagittarius

Although today may prove to be somewhat quieter than yesterday, in the light of yesterday's horoscope you are hardly likely to grumble about it! The fact is that you have been working really hard at life, and everyone needs a break now and again, even Leo. Spend some time with family members or friends you really like.

4 FRIDAY
Moon Age Day 25   Moon Sign Capricorn

Personal issues from the past are inclined to take up too much time today. Put such matters on the back burner whenever you can at present and concentrate for the moment on what is needed right now. It isn't often Leo people become confused but it is possible under the prevailing circumstances.

5 SATURDAY   *Moon Age Day 26   Moon Sign Capricorn*

Interests that allow your imagination to run free are definitely the ones you should be considering at the moment. There are a few limitations around in a practical sense and it will not be possible to address all of these. Better by far to sit back and do something different for a while if it is at all possible.

6 SUNDAY   *Moon Age Day 27   Moon Sign Aquarius*

With the 'lunar low' around, everyday progress is slowed – almost to a standstill. Instead of worrying about this situation, use it to your advantage. When things can't be done the best way forward is to wait. In the meantime you have a couple of days when it is possible to stand and watch the flowers grow. That's good for you.

7 MONDAY   *Moon Age Day 28   Moon Sign Aquarius*

Suspend all decision making and let others take control, at least for today. There can be great contentment in seeing people succeeding as a result of the very real help and advice you have offered them in the past. There is time to achieve everything you wish but today isn't that time. Socially speaking life should be fun.

8 TUESDAY   *Moon Age Day 0   Moon Sign Pisces*

This really isn't the best time for grandiose schemes of any sort. Energy is not as easy to come by right now so you may find that a little careful thought is more use than any amount of direct effort. If you mull things over carefully it should be possible to get your own way in most matters.

9 WEDNESDAY   *Moon Age Day 1   Moon Sign Pisces*

If you use your initiative at the moment, professional developments may be the result. Most aspects of life should be going your way and there are people around you who actively want to help the process. Rules and regulations could threaten to get on your nerves but in the main you tend to ignore them now.

10 THURSDAY — *Moon Age Day 2   Moon Sign Aries*

It looks as though romance is more likely to be on the cards than has been the case for quite some time. Don't be too quick to make a move, however. Everything comes to he or she who waits patiently and this is certainly true for you now. Today may involve a good deal of planning for the weekend ahead.

11 FRIDAY — *Moon Age Day 3   Moon Sign Aries*

Planetary trends continue to favour using your initiative at work in order to make professional advances. These trends may also have a positive influence on other areas of your life and help you to get along with those around you. Use these influences to your advantage and don't allow any negative input to dissuade you.

12 SATURDAY — *Moon Age Day 4   Moon Sign Taurus*

This continues to be quite a fruitful period for friendship, mainly on account of the present position of Venus in your solar chart. At the same time you should notice that personal attachments have a stronger and more meaningful importance. Just about anyone can be helpful now, though that's because of your own attitude.

13 SUNDAY — *Moon Age Day 5   Moon Sign Taurus*

It's the weekend, so you can't expect to make the sort of professional progress that has been so clearly marked during this week. Instead, why not leave yourself with the time to enjoy a relaxing interlude? This doesn't mean that you have to stand still. Physical activity is to be encouraged right now.

14 MONDAY — *Moon Age Day 6   Moon Sign Gemini*

'Grace under pressure' is the best attitude to take when it comes to sorting out slight hiccups in your personal life. At least you are turning your attention in the direction of romance, and there hasn't been a lot of time for that of late. At work you are probably showing a few anxieties, which is not to be recommended now.

15 TUESDAY *Moon Age Day 7   Moon Sign Gemini*

There is good scope for a little monetary increase at present. Look at your incomings and outgoings carefully because you are likely to find that you are better off than you previously thought. Finding the time to explain things may not be easy but you are likely to have more patience than usual and that should help.

16 WEDNESDAY *Moon Age Day 8   Moon Sign Gemini*

The potential for success is fairly strong, the only real stumbling block being keeping your friends working so keenly on your behalf. Where practical and financial projects are concerned, you are going to have to find some way to convince others that they are working towards their own betterment too.

17 THURSDAY *Moon Age Day 9   Moon Sign Cancer*

Intellectually speaking, an intense view of life means you could so easily become obsessed with matters that are not really very important. Take a step back and look at things rationally. If you are suffering from some minor physical ailment, you may need to look at your working practices, which could hold the solution to the problem.

18 FRIDAY *Moon Age Day 10   Moon Sign Cancer*

This could be a good time to have a break from some of the obligations that may have been weighing heavily on you of late. With the Moon in your solar twelfth house, you are given to being more contemplative. A quiet time, spent with relatives or friends, might complete the picture in the evening.

19 SATURDAY *Moon Age Day 11   Moon Sign Leo*

This is the time of the month when it is possible for you to talk anyone into anything. Don't be afraid to put your own point of view forward or to be as positive as your go-ahead zodiac sign allows you to be. The 'lunar high' offers new incentives and brings a desire to make progress in every way.

20 SUNDAY
Moon Age Day 12   Moon Sign Leo

Energy and enthusiasm remain generally high, as does your desire to help other people in just about any way you can. Some caution may be necessary when dealing with those who are not as dynamic as you are. However, what's really important is to lead by example and that won't be difficult today.

21 MONDAY
Moon Age Day 13   Moon Sign Virgo

You discover today that there is certainly more than one way to get ahead. With a wealth of new projects about to be launched, the only real problem now is finding enough time to get everything done. This difficulty can be addressed by getting other people involved from the start.

22 TUESDAY
Moon Age Day 14   Moon Sign Virgo

You can spend so much time thinking about the future today that you get very little done in the present. It is vitally important in at least some situations to keep your eye firmly on the ball. When it comes to having fun, you should not encounter many obstacles at all. Simply find a friend and pitch in.

23 WEDNESDAY
Moon Age Day 15   Moon Sign Virgo

Things that are happening on the domestic scene may not be wonderful or inviting at this time. It is probably for this reason that you are spending more time working, or socially with friends. Don't turn away from your family altogether though. There is someone close who really needs a listening ear now.

24 THURSDAY
Moon Age Day 16   Moon Sign Libra

You are quite a dynamo at the moment, though that does not mean you will fail to become tired by the relentless pace you are setting yourself. At the first sign of stress, you need to slow down and to take stock. Solace can come from the direction of your partner, with whom an extra-special closeness now exists.

25 FRIDAY   *Moon Age Day 17   Moon Sign Libra*

Some of the ways you choose to solve personal problems are unique to say the least. It might be suggested that you are somewhat unrealistic at the moment, though you would doubtless disagree. In the end, you are more or less forced to do things your own way. You can't help it; it's called being a Leo.

26 SATURDAY   *Moon Age Day 18   Moon Sign Scorpio*

Now is the time to genuinely assess what is going on in your life and to make a few minor alterations, especially with regard to professional matters. It is possible that you may meet up with people from the past, some of whom could have a fairly important part to play in your thinking for the future.

27 SUNDAY   *Moon Age Day 19   Moon Sign Scorpio*

The Sun is now in your solar ninth house and along comes a chance to broaden your horizons generally and to get into new projects. Romance can lighten the day no end, as can social gatherings involving people you like a great deal. Beware a slight tendency at present to try to shirk certain responsibilities.

28 MONDAY   *Moon Age Day 20   Moon Sign Scorpio*

Now is the time to get your foot down on the professional accelerator. You know what you want from life, and have a pretty good idea how you should go about getting it. There are details today that must not be left to chance and you cannot afford to take the chance that they will sort themselves out.

29 TUESDAY   *Moon Age Day 21   Moon Sign Sagittarius*

Getting on with others might not be too easy. If you want to make certain that there are no hiccups in relationships today, you need to stay close to those individuals who know you well and who are invariably on your side. You may begin to question some aspects of your social circle around now.

30 WEDNESDAY · *Moon Age Day 22* · *Moon Sign Sagittarius*

You could find yourself in the right place at the right time to make a financial killing of some sort. This situation could easily be linked with medium and long-term planning from the past, which is finally maturing. Don't be too quick to judge the actions of a friend without checking matters with them.

31 THURSDAY · *Moon Age Day 23* · *Moon Sign Capricorn*

Along comes a period when it seems vitally important to widen your horizons. It could be that you are only now waking up to the changing year and noticing that spring is in the air. The position of the Sun in your chart is the main driving force behind this mood and it demands change of some sort.

April

2016

1 FRIDAY
Moon Age Day 24   Moon Sign Capricorn

Emotional relationships need some careful handling today, probably because certain people are over-sensitive at the moment. When it comes to getting things done in a general sense you should have little trouble, though it may be necessary to alter your routines quite a bit for a few days.

2 SATURDAY
Moon Age Day 25   Moon Sign Capricorn

It is possible that you will be thrust into the social limelight today much more than you may have been expecting. Take such situations in your stride and try not to react too much to the fact that everyone wants your opinion. It is at least good to know that you are popular and that your views count for so much.

3 SUNDAY
Moon Age Day 26   Moon Sign Aquarius

With the 'lunar low' around it's time to slow things down somewhat. This is hardly likely to come as any sort of shock to your system. On the contrary, after so many busy days it will probably feel good to allow others to take the strain more. Routines can be dealt with quite easily today and tomorrow.

4 MONDAY
Moon Age Day 27   Moon Sign Aquarius

It is unlikely that you will choose to push yourself any more than is absolutely necessary whilst the Moon is in your opposite zodiac sign of Aquarius. Enjoy some of the benefits of past efforts and do what you can to support family members, some of whom will be pleased you have the time to talk to them.

5 TUESDAY
Moon Age Day 28   Moon Sign Pisces

Practical matters will often seem to be labours of love today. You clearly know what you want from life, even if it isn't always possible to achieve your objectives in full. There should be plenty of people around to tell you how wonderful you are – a massage of the ego that is usually welcome to Leo.

6 WEDNESDAY
Moon Age Day 29   Moon Sign Pisces

The right kind of opportunities now seem to come along quite readily, sometimes without you even having to do anything to inspire them. What really matters today is personal incentive, together with your ability to force situations forward, even on those occasions when others are trying to block you.

7 THURSDAY
Moon Age Day 0   Moon Sign Aries

Friendly co-operation and a boost to your personal popularity seem to be the hallmarks of this period. This stage of the week brings new incentives, some of which are being offered by people who haven't seemed to like you much in the past. Get some rest later in the day, in the company of loved ones.

8 FRIDAY
Moon Age Day 1   Moon Sign Aries

The company of like-minded colleagues can prove to be extremely stimulating at present. Getting what you want from life, especially in a professional sense, really should not be too difficult, though you need to be certain that there are moments left in which you can forget practicalities in favour of personal contentment.

9 SATURDAY
Moon Age Day 2   Moon Sign Taurus

You may still not be working towards new incentives or showing how dynamic you can be – you simply are not in that sort of mood. What could be fun would be to undertake some sort of trip, most likely with loved ones or friends. You might prefer to take some time out to fully register the arrival of spring.

10 SUNDAY   *Moon Age Day 3   Moon Sign Taurus*

Today could prove to be good for all practical matters. Holding on to what you have is likely to seem quite important at this stage, though it is possible to try too hard. New opportunities may arise if you work today. The offer of changed or enhanced responsibilities also cannot be ruled out.

11 MONDAY   *Moon Age Day 4   Moon Sign Gemini*

A beneficial high-energy phase continues at the start of this new working week, allowing you to get a great deal done and to show a very positive face to the world at large. Attitude is all-important when it comes to prospective changes at work, though general relationships should seem fairly settled.

12 TUESDAY   *Moon Age Day 5   Moon Sign Gemini*

There are some challenges around today, particularly in terms of social contacts. Instead of rising to these as a matter of course it would be better for the moment to simply wait and see. What matters most today is the realisation that you are in charge of your own destiny and that others cannot rule your life.

13 WEDNESDAY   *Moon Age Day 6   Moon Sign Cancer*

On the financial front you can expect greater feelings of security now and a better ability to see things going your way. Tackling specific jobs might prove to be somewhat awkward under present trends, which is why you have much more to gain by simply allowing yourself to have as much fun as possible.

14 THURSDAY   *Moon Age Day 7   Moon Sign Cancer*

Much seems to centre around the need to be practical at the moment. This isn't particularly difficult for you, but it won't be easy to keep this head on all the time. Social situations call too and especially if you are a young Leo you will feel a great need to be out and about, having fun.

15 FRIDAY
Moon Age Day 8   Moon Sign Leo

Now is the time to make a powerful impression on the world. The Moon is back in your sign and there is everything to play for. Leave behind the slower qualities of the last couple of days and be willing to tell the world how you feel. There ought to be many people around who have your best interests at heart.

16 SATURDAY
Moon Age Day 9   Moon Sign Leo

Once again you can expect to be the centre of attention and to make your own luck as you go along. Routines really don't matter to you at present. All that you are concerned with is getting the job done. Later in the day you should be watching out for romantic interludes that really put the icing on the cake.

17 SUNDAY
Moon Age Day 10   Moon Sign Virgo

You are now entering a period of escapism. This is uncommon for Leo and you need to be careful that you do not neglect important jobs you have already started but still require your attention. All the same, there is nothing wrong with being a dreamer now and again. You might even arrive at some startling conclusions.

18 MONDAY
Moon Age Day 11   Moon Sign Virgo

It is true that you can be quite impressionable at the moment but that means you could also be hoodwinked if you are not careful. Listen to what is being said to you and consider the words carefully. It may be equally important to read documents through to discover what is contained in the small print.

19 TUESDAY
Moon Age Day 12   Moon Sign Virgo

This should be a rewarding day, not least of all because your sense of adventure is going off the scale. Don't put off until tomorrow anything that you know in your heart you can complete easily now. Routines may not be interesting, but even these can be undertaken with a smile if you put your mind to it.

20 WEDNESDAY · *Moon Age Day 13*   *Moon Sign Libra*

Handling several different tasks at the same time should be a piece of cake today. Don't allow yourself to be diverted from the path you know to be right for you and insist on getting your own way on those occasions when you just know that your intuition is sound. Look out for kind words coming your way later in the day.

21 THURSDAY · *Moon Age Day 14*   *Moon Sign Libra*

You should be happily on the go and keen to keep up as high a profile as you possibly can. Following on from the trends of yesterday it is important at the moment not to leave jobs unfinished. So many practical necessities crowd in on you today that it might be difficult to see the wood for the trees.

22 FRIDAY · *Moon Age Day 15*   *Moon Sign Libra*

There are great opportunities around now to broaden your horizons in a general sense. Whether or not you choose to actually do anything specific today remains to be seen. Certainly any better weather will encourage you to get out of the house and journeys of all sorts are well highlighted at present.

23 SATURDAY ☿ *Moon Age Day 16*   *Moon Sign Scorpio*

There may be a few setbacks today in a career sense. Take these in your stride and make the best of them. You will still be on top form in your social life and unlikely to get on the wrong side of the people who are important to you. Avoid the temptation to spend too much cash at the start of the weekend.

24 SUNDAY ☿ *Moon Age Day 17*   *Moon Sign Scorpio*

Some tasks will still appear to be an uphill struggle at the beginning of the day but the pace will soon alter. As the afternoon gives way to the evening your confidence should grow rapidly. At this time you turn your attention towards those people who are the most important in your life as a whole.

25 MONDAY ☿ *Moon Age Day 18   Moon Sign Sagittarius*

Some hopeful news may arrive today regarding your present objectives, and particularly so on a personal level. This is a Monday of genuine opportunity and a time that offers you moments of real inspiration. Don't waste time trying to sort out the world. Look after your own affairs for now at least.

26 TUESDAY ☿ *Moon Age Day 19   Moon Sign Sagittarius*

You may find that others are all too happy to follow your lead today. That's fine as long as things work out to their advantage. Take care not to give an all-knowing impression if in reality you are guessing somewhat. It may be the case that comfort and security means more to those around you than to you now.

27 WEDNESDAY ☿ *Moon Age Day 20   Moon Sign Capricorn*

A continued boost to all matters practical and professional is possible whilst the Sun now stands so firmly in your solar tenth house. Today offers variety, together with the chance to look at old matters in a new way. Flexibility is the key to success in social settings and loving partnerships.

28 THURSDAY ☿ *Moon Age Day 21   Moon Sign Capricorn*

This period positively affect all relationships, whether they are close or more distant. It should not be difficult to communicate with the world at large and you are unlikely to lock yourself behind your own castle walls right now. A long-term project needs careful thought, but perhaps also the input of a friend.

29 FRIDAY ☿ *Moon Age Day 22   Moon Sign Capricorn*

It is unlikely that you will find too much time or space for relaxation right now. The weekend brings a greater sense of ease but for now so many of you will want to finish the working week with a flourish. Concentrate on romantic encounters and by the evening you should be telling someone how important they are to you.

30 SATURDAY ☿ *Moon Age Day 23* *Moon Sign Aquarius*

It is likely that professional matters are now on a roll. Whatever you do for a living, you are now in a position to do it to the best of your ability. Meanwhile you need to be sure that your social life is not losing out. Romance is on the cards this Saturday, particularly for young or young-at heart-Leos.

May

2016

1 SUNDAY
☿ *Moon Age Day 24   Moon Sign Aquarius*

Getting along with others certainly does not have to be a battle today, but you may see it as such at times. Listen carefully to what is being said to you, keeping your own opinions on hold until you have done so. In the end you may well realise that your views are broadly the same as those of others.

2 MONDAY
☿   *Moon Age Day 25   Moon Sign Pisces*

The acquisition of money is one of your great skills right now. That means you will be trying hard to make gains, both inside and outside of work. Try not to take on two things at once because you will get on much better at this time if you simply concentrate on the job you are actually doing.

3 TUESDAY
☿   *Moon Age Day 26   Moon Sign Pisces*

Happiness to you at the moment is likely to mean being on the move. An early holiday would suit you just fine but if this isn't possible, try to vary your routines as much as you can. Avoid staying in the same place for too long and make sure that variety is also a strong characteristic of your social life.

4 WEDNESDAY
☿   *Moon Age Day 27   Moon Sign Aries*

Friendships and group encounters take on a particularly pleasant atmosphere right now. You are feeling confident, and this is the component that makes the difference between a happy and a miserable Leo subject. In a positive and creative mood, you may find you are thinking about changes regarding your home.

5 THURSDAY ☿ *Moon Age Day 28   Moon Sign Aries*

There is important news about now, and though you may not be in the best position to take advantage of it, this is a period when it would be quite sensible to keep your ears open. By tomorrow, you will be champing at the bit and anxious to get on. Just for today you tend to be in more of a planning mode.

6 FRIDAY ☿ *Moon Age Day 0   Moon Sign Taurus*

Financial matters should be looking stronger as the day goes on. Although you may be in a position to gamble a little, some circumspection will also be necessary. New ideas could be coming your way at any time now and you will probably be willing to listen to the advice of good friends. Socially speaking you will want to be active.

7 SATURDAY ☿ *Moon Age Day 1   Moon Sign Taurus*

What a wonderful time this would be for getting on the right side of your boss, so it is a shame that many Leo people will not be at work today. Nevertheless, you can influence others positively, even in your social and family life. Everything comes together to make you charming, yet decisive and determined.

8 SUNDAY ☿ *Moon Age Day 2   Moon Sign Gemini*

Some information you receive today could turn out to be very valuable. There are enlightening times ahead and maybe a meeting with people who will eventually be of great value in your life. Existing pals want to spend time with you, but there are choices to be made at a time when you are so busy.

9 MONDAY ☿ *Moon Age Day 3   Moon Sign Gemini*

There could be a lot of potentially useful information coming your way right now. On the personal front, relationships are looking especially good and there could not be a better time than this for speaking words of love to someone who is extra special. The kinder and gentler side of your nature is now on display.

10 TUESDAY ☿ *Moon Age Day 4   Moon Sign Cancer*

It takes a lot of courage to admit that you might have been wrong. If you have to eat a little humble pie at some stage today, make sure you do so with a good heart. It would be better to say nothing than to be grudging in your apology. Those who know you well may have some words of wisdom later.

11 WEDNESDAY ☿ *Moon Age Day 5   Moon Sign Cancer*

There is no doubt that you display considerable charm right now. This should be noticeable to almost everyone you come across, which means a boost to your personal popularity. Look after money carefully, particularly later in the day, when you may be faced with a bargain that looks just too good to be true.

12 THURSDAY ☿ *Moon Age Day 6   Moon Sign Leo*

Thursday brings positive aspects to bear on you. With plenty of energy and a great desire to get on, the amount you actually get through can be breathtaking. Avoid family arguments and stay out there in the mainstream of life. That is where you will feel most comfortable and the place you make the greatest impression.

13 FRIDAY ☿ *Moon Age Day 7   Moon Sign Leo*

Friday's trends suggest a continuation of the generally favourable influences surrounding you at present. Although there is plenty to be done, you approach all jobs with a cheerful attitude. If there is a need in your life at the moment to specifically tell others how they should behave, this might be a good day to speak out.

14 SATURDAY ☿ *Moon Age Day 8   Moon Sign Leo*

Today should offer you the chance to come good on promises you have made previously. The influence exerted by the position of Mars in your chart means that you will direct your positive actions towards matters in the house and home. Keep an open mind about proffered changes on the work front and don't dismiss offers of new responsibilities.

15 SUNDAY ☿ *Moon Age Day 9 Moon Sign Virgo*

Your spirits might not be quite as high as you would wish but that doesn't mean you are slowing down. It may be that you simply don't have quite your usual level of self-confidence, though this situation will change soon enough. By the evening, you will probably be in the right frame of mind to party.

16 MONDAY ☿ *Moon Age Day 10 Moon Sign Virgo*

This would be a good time to make sure you have your eyes and ears open because there is a good deal of fresh input coming along today. You might also feel the need of some fresh air and certainly will not take kindly to being cooped up all day long. A certain restless streak may begin to develop.

17 TUESDAY ☿ *Moon Age Day 11 Moon Sign Libra*

The emphasis today is on the wider social world and it is just possible that your work will take something of a back seat. You probably have a few inspirational ideas in your head and will want to get a few of them moving in the real world. It may be a good idea to look for some support right now.

18 WEDNESDAY ☿ *Moon Age Day 12 Moon Sign Libra*

Enjoying all that domestic relationships have to offer you could prove somewhat more difficult than usual today. The fact is that you won't get on with everyone at home right now. From your point of view, it may seem that someone is being distinctly difficult, but it is possible you should be looking in the mirror!

19 THURSDAY ☿ *Moon Age Day 13 Moon Sign Libra*

A more carefree influence comes along, thanks to the position of Mercury in your solar chart. This is certainly likely to be positive in terms of your communication skills and also enhances your desire to do things in a very spontaneous manner. Friends should be happy to join in today.

20 FRIDAY   ☿   *Moon Age Day 14   Moon Sign Scorpio*

This would not be the best day to chance your arm, or to take on tasks that you know are going to be especially difficult. Keep life light and easy, settling for quiet times and leaving all major decisions until later. If you obey these few rules, you can have quite an enjoyable twenty-four hours.

21 SATURDAY   ☿   *Moon Age Day 15   Moon Sign Scorpio*

The chances of success in a general sense are a good deal stronger today. Almost immediately you pick up the traces of issues that were important to you before yesterday came along. Chasing details is a piece of cake and it is very unlikely that anyone could fool you at present.

22 SUNDAY   ☿ *Moon Age Day 16   Moon Sign Sagittarius*

This is a time when you will benefit from broadening your intellectual and social interests. Outings for pleasure are indicated and your desire to experience cultural pursuits may be enhanced. If you work on a Sunday you may want to consider taking a day's leave to make the best of these trends.

23 MONDAY   *Moon Age Day 17   Moon Sign Sagittarius*

You need to treat this day with some respect. It won't help if you insist on doing practical things or even domestic chores to the extent that you drive yourself mad with them. What really works today is some diversity and a little excitement. You have strong enough powers of persuasion to get others to join in.

24 TUESDAY   *Moon Age Day 18   Moon Sign Sagittarius*

Maximise your potential today by being a true Leo. You can afford to be bold and fearless, partly because you retain another Leo quality – a sense of honour. You won't do anything today that materially or personally works against the best interests of others. Like the monarch that your sign represents, you watch over your subjects.

25 WEDNESDAY   *Moon Age Day 19   Moon Sign Capricorn*

What a good time this would be for family gatherings of almost any sort. You are very sociable at present and can even put up cheerfully with the one or two individuals you may not care for very much. Keep an open mind about a change in travel plans that will have a bearing on you later.

26 THURSDAY   *Moon Age Day 20   Moon Sign Capricorn*

You will most certainly end up in an undesirable situation if you put your trust in the wrong people today, so it is vitally important that you take nothing at all for granted. Instead you should be more cautious than usual and ensure that you ask the most searching of questions, especially regarding contracts.

27 FRIDAY   *Moon Age Day 21   Moon Sign Aquarius*

This probably will not be the most dynamic Friday you have ever lived through, though the peace and quiet may be of your choice rather than something imposed upon you. Spend time with those you love, and with interesting people who may come into your life for the first time. Accept that your levels of physical energy won't be at a peak.

28 SATURDAY   *Moon Age Day 22   Moon Sign Aquarius*

Ordinary progress is possible today but anything beyond that is bound to be rather difficult. Once the 'lunar low' is out of the way you will move forward progressively. In the meantime you will have to make do with second best. Remain social and spend as much time as possible with relatives and good friends.

29 SUNDAY   *Moon Age Day 23   Moon Sign Pisces*

There are a few emotional setbacks today, and these should be strictly guarded against if at all possible. Routines are not for you on this Sunday and you could do with a change of scene. The summer is approaching and you would respond positively to a trip out somewhere, maybe into the country.

30 MONDAY
Moon Age Day 24   Moon Sign Pisces

All of a sudden, and seemingly out of the blue, your persuasive powers are off the scale today. You are noisier, but more rewarding to have around and show far more confidence in your own judgement than was the case during the weekend. Several trends contribute to this mood, so make use of them.

31 TUESDAY
Moon Age Day 25   Moon Sign Pisces

This is likely to be a very busy day. Negotiations and communications generally are the area of life that interests you specifically and you won't take too kindly to anyone who appears to throw a spanner in the works. You should find time to entertain family members and to make a fuss of your partner.

2016

1 WEDNESDAY   *Moon Age Day 26   Moon Sign Aries*

Professional matters, though containing a few little ups and downs at present, should be running generally smoothly as far as you are concerned. The most fulfilling moments today could come from personal attachments and it is possible that you will discover one or two admirers you didn't know you had.

2 THURSDAY   *Moon Age Day 27   Moon Sign Aries*

Social matters continue to bring a degree of light relief to your life and help you to redress the balance, since matters at work could be somewhat more complicated than of late. Concentrate on having a good time and don't ask too much of yourself on those occasions when lightness of touch is what counts.

3 FRIDAY   *Moon Age Day 28   Moon Sign Taurus*

Follow through on recent proposals and if today offers any free time, consider some ideas that are in the offing now. Domestic issues could demand your attention too, especially the situations of family members who may not appear to be particularly happy. Avoid undue stress and try to make Friday happy all round.

4 SATURDAY   *Moon Age Day 0   Moon Sign Taurus*

Your daily life should continue in an interesting and informative way. With your eyes firmly open to many of the opportunities that life presently has on offer, give yourself a pat on the back for recent successes. You seem to be especially social right now and would probably enjoy some extra time spent with friends.

5 SUNDAY
Moon Age Day 1   Moon Sign Gemini

You are easily able to bring out the best in others today and social get togethers look particularly interesting. If you work at the weekend, you are likely to find yourself being sought out by people who are not as sure of themselves as you tend to be. Acting with confidence is all-important today and feathers your nest for later.

6 MONDAY
Moon Age Day 2   Moon Sign Gemini

Your working routines might be beset by communication difficulties of one sort or another. It isn't so much that you are failing to say the right thing, more that those around you hear what they want to hear. All the same it is worth thinking carefully before you commit yourself to any specific course of action.

7 TUESDAY
Moon Age Day 3   Moon Sign Cancer

What you get from group situations at the moment could prove to be most rewarding later. You are able to see the good in almost any situation and also have the measure of those around you. For now Leo shows a good deal of patience, which has to be an advantage when dealing with a world of people who sometimes make mistakes.

8 WEDNESDAY
Moon Age Day 4   Moon Sign Cancer

Be careful not to spend too much today and as a result leave yourself short of cash later. Routines are easily dealt with, leaving you time to enjoy a full and happy social life, probably in the company of people whose presence in your life you relish. Comfort and security take an especially central role in your day.

9 THURSDAY
Moon Age Day 5   Moon Sign Leo

Lady Luck is likely to be with you as you embark on a very fruitful period. Put your energy to work in a professional sense, whilst at the same time keeping your options open in a social sense. Even personal relationships come under the spotlight today and you push forward on practically every front of your life.

10 FRIDAY
Moon Age Day 6   Moon Sign Leo

This is certainly not a particularly quiet sort of Friday for many Leo subjects. The 'lunar high' finds you willing to have a go at almost anything and more talkative than has been the case for a number of days. If there are any frustrations today they stem from the potentially restrictive boundaries that might prevail.

11 SATURDAY
Moon Age Day 7   Moon Sign Virgo

Keep a sense of proportion regarding issues that are not really as important as you may once have believed. There is plenty to keep you occupied and a real chance to make progress in matters that have stuck fast recently. Close personal relationships are apt to come under the spotlight of your attention today.

12 SUNDAY
Moon Age Day 8   Moon Sign Virgo

Today it is towards domestic arrangements that your mind is likely to turn. A good deal of happiness is possible, mainly engendered by those closest to you. Expecting a day during which no mistakes are made could be over optimistic, yet it is obvious that most of the steps you take are sensible and productive.

13 MONDAY
Moon Age Day 9   Moon Sign Virgo

There is too little time for fun and enjoyment today. With a thousand things to get done, and maybe nobody around to help share the load, you are inclined to dash around from pillar to post in a way that is not exactly helpful. A little forward planning could ease the situation to a great extent.

14 TUESDAY
Moon Age Day 10   Moon Sign Libra

In terms of practical involvement in life you are second to none now. This can be quite a startling day, just as long as you handle it right from the start. Get on with what pleases you and do everything to the very best of your ability. There are plenty of opportunities to shine when in company.

15 WEDNESDAY   *Moon Age Day 11   Moon Sign Libra*

People actively seem to want to do you favours today. This could be because you are smiling so much and putting yourself out on their behalf without even realising the fact. You may also be on the receiving end of some simple good luck, which may bode well for significant success in meetings and discussions.

16 THURSDAY   *Moon Age Day 12   Moon Sign Scorpio*

What you learn today about yourself can be both rewarding and eye-opening. Mostly this will come from the direction of family and friends. In most situations you tend to sell yourself short this month, so it will be good to realise that you have all the support in the world when you feel you need it the most.

17 FRIDAY   *Moon Age Day 13   Moon Sign Scorpio*

Career interests can be slightly upset by present attitudes. Not all of these are going to be yours but even when others are involved your own point of view counts. Try to remain patient and don't take prohibitive action against situations that will resolve themselves if you are only patient.

18 SATURDAY   *Moon Age Day 14   Moon Sign Scorpio*

Work and material gains could prove less stimulating now, though of course this is the weekend and as a result your mind is likely to be turning in different directions. Take some time to please yourself, particularly in the company of people you know and like. Romance is on the cards for most Leo subjects today.

19 SUNDAY   *Moon Age Day 15   Moon Sign Sagittarius*

It looks as though you will enjoy being in the limelight at the moment and there is a possibility that others are putting you on some sort of pedestal. There are people in the world who would find this state of affairs uncomfortable. Fortunately you are not one of them and can rise to the occasion easily.

20 MONDAY   *Moon Age Day 16   Moon Sign Sagittarius*

A potentially wonderful time for social interests, even though work will be taking up at least a proportion of the day. Do your best to have a good time, and as much as possible in the company of loved ones. Balancing the needs of a practical life and a personal one is the juggling act for the moment.

21 TUESDAY   *Moon Age Day 17   Moon Sign Capricorn*

A joint financial issue requires a cool head and a great deal of common sense. Although you are unlikely to agree with the way things are going, you won't wish to offer any offence. As a result you need to talk things through carefully and to be as diplomatic as your present nature will allow.

22 WEDNESDAY   *Moon Age Day 18   Moon Sign Capricorn*

Maybe this is a time when you should be opting for something different. You don't want to start feeling that life is passing you by. Your own actions are what count right now, together with an ability to get things done by allying your talent. Someone very close to you might just have a startling idea.

23 THURSDAY   *Moon Age Day 19   Moon Sign Aquarius*

A few disappointments are possible today, thanks to the arrival of the 'lunar low'. Of course if you are in the right frame of mind to start the day this is much less likely. Check matters carefully and don't bite off more than you can realistically chew. There should be help on offer if you are looking for it.

24 FRIDAY   *Moon Age Day 20   Moon Sign Aquarius*

Although energy may still be in short supply there is no reason at all why today should prove to be essentially disappointing. There is time to think about matters and that's what the 'lunar low' is all about. Simply stick to what you know and allow yourself some time to recharge overworked batteries.

25 SATURDAY   *Moon Age Day 21   Moon Sign Aquarius*

This is a very favourable period for socialising and an altogether happy sort of Saturday for most Leo subjects. Try to do something different and take account of the turning year by getting out of the house. Be bold in your endeavours, though leaving room for the opinions and actions of those around you.

26 SUNDAY   *Moon Age Day 22   Moon Sign Pisces*

Your social life is likely to be on a roll today. If there have been slightly negative influences these are now retreating, leaving you feeling much more like your old self. You want to join in with almost anything and can certainly be the life and soul of the party. Avoid making pointless mistakes if you are at work.

27 MONDAY   *Moon Age Day 23   Moon Sign Pisces*

Don't try to please too many people today – one or two is quite sufficient for the moment. You can't be all things to all people and it's a waste of time trying. There is nothing at all wrong with your aims and objectives, simply the way you are trying to put them into practice. Some careful thought is necessary.

28 TUESDAY   *Moon Age Day 24   Moon Sign Aries*

Work life is likely to be little more than business as usual at this stage of the working week. It is within the realm of your personal life that most of the potential excitement lies. You should be deeply romantic at this time and more than willing to let your partner – or a prospective one – know how you feel.

29 WEDNESDAY   *Moon Age Day 25   Moon Sign Aries*

Though career matters probably have you on the hop today, in more personal situations you are responding extremely well. You can get a number of jobs out of the way very early in the day, leaving yourself time later to think things through more carefully. Take advantage of some extra help.

30 THURSDAY   *Moon Age Day 26   Moon Sign Taurus*

If you have to decide anything major, consult with someone you trust first. This second opinion might not prove to be strictly necessary but it will be reassuring. Don't dwell unnecessarily on your perceived limitations, but instead have confidence. This is a day when you need to feel equal to the task because that is exactly what you are.

July
2016

1 FRIDAY
Moon Age Day 27   Moon Sign Taurus

The planets suggest that your focus is on a settled and happy family life at present, and this is therefore the direction in which your mind tends to turn. Gradually the forces at work within your chart will begin to speed things up but for today at least you are able to balance work and play well and you continue to enjoy natural affection.

2 SATURDAY
Moon Age Day 28   Moon Sign Gemini

You may find that there is a limit to the number of people you are able to charm today. Avoid coming over as being insincere, especially when you are dealing with individuals you know to be deeply perceptive. What counts the most is honesty, even if you sense that certain people don't like the real you.

3 SUNDAY
Moon Age Day 29   Moon Sign Gemini

This is a good period for building on recent successes and for letting others know that you are equal to just about any task. Work hard, but be willing to enjoy yourself fully once the requirements of the working day are over and done with. It should be possible to turn a difficult situation fully to your advantage.

4 MONDAY
Moon Age Day 0   Moon Sign Cancer

If there are setbacks in your career today you will need to take them in your stride. Luckily, trends suggest that you should find it easier than usual to simply shrug your shoulders and not to overreact to any situation. The best way to show others how things should be done is now definitely by example.

5 TUESDAY   *Moon Age Day 1   Moon Sign Cancer*

Your love life tends to continue in a very lively manner. Meanwhile your persuasive skills come very much into their own, allowing you to get your own way in situations that have not been to your advantage recently. Avoid getting stuck in any sort of rut socially and be prepared to ring the changes frequently now.

6 WEDNESDAY   *Moon Age Day 2   Moon Sign Leo*

With the middle of the week should come the mental and physical peak associated with the 'lunar high'. Not everyone is equally helpful today but that doesn't really matter. Once you have the bit between your teeth it's upward and onwards, whether or not you receive the sort of support you might have come to expect.

7 THURSDAY   *Moon Age Day 3   Moon Sign Leo*

There seems to be a very generous spirit in the air today and you have a good ability to get what you want from almost any situation. Of course you won't find the world and its population universally helpful. What you do have right now is a great skill in picking out those people who will fall in line with your ideas.

8 FRIDAY   *Moon Age Day 4   Moon Sign Virgo*

You could find yourself diverted by an issue from the past, which would be a shame at the end of a working week when you have much to do. Talk to people who are in the know and tell them just exactly how you feel about any given situation. You should be quite persuasive in personal matters.

9 SATURDAY   *Moon Age Day 5   Moon Sign Virgo*

Entertainment is on your mind. You know how to enjoy yourself and it will be easy to find people who are like-minded. All work and no play makes Leo a dull person, so drop the traces of responsibility from time to time and concentrate on having fun. Routines can be dealt with by other people for a change.

10 SUNDAY   *Moon Age Day 6   Moon Sign Virgo*

What is happening at home ought to encourage the lazier side of your nature to take over. Why not, it is Sunday after all? Even Leo can't burn the candle at both ends indefinitely. Be prepared to put your feet up and to spend time talking to those who may not see you anywhere near as often as they would wish.

11 MONDAY   *Moon Age Day 7   Moon Sign Libra*

This is a day when you should enjoy getting down to brass tacks. The practical world may need far more attention than you have given it during the last week or so, though turning to such matters should now be second nature. Avoid pointless discussions about situations that have no substance in the real world.

12 TUESDAY   *Moon Age Day 8   Moon Sign Libra*

There could be a reunion of some sort today with a person you haven't seen for quite some time. The past is probably on your mind a good deal and it is possible to put something right now that has been amiss for quite a while. On the practical front you appear to have the ability to get a great deal done.

13 WEDNESDAY   *Moon Age Day 9   Moon Sign Scorpio*

You tend to be bolder than ever at present and will be quite keen to take a few chances. That is fine, just as long as the risks are calculated carefully. Where you should avoid them altogether is with regard to money. If you have documents to sign at present, read the small print carefully.

14 THURSDAY   *Moon Age Day 10   Moon Sign Scorpio*

You will want to be on the move today and so will not take kindly to any situation that ties you exclusively to a particular spot. Give yourself a pat on the back for recent successes at work but do not allow these to go to your head. There is still plenty to do if you want to get exactly where you need to be.

15 FRIDAY   *Moon Age Day 11   Moon Sign Scorpio*

With the Sun in your solar twelfth house, there is an inclination to see the down side of life from time to time. With other planetary contacts now in operation, today could be such a period. Try not to get depressed, particularly regarding issues that could so easily resolve themselves in the longer-term.

16 SATURDAY   *Moon Age Day 12   Moon Sign Sagittarius*

Outside elements could so easily prevent you from getting an important message across right now. You can strive and struggle to say the right thing, but the wrong words are apt to come out. Keep a sense of proportion and, if at all possible, laugh at your own slight inadequacy today.

17 SUNDAY   *Moon Age Day 13   Moon Sign Sagittarius*

You are likely to enjoy being on the go from morning until night this Sunday, though once again you would gain by staying away from situations that mean 'working' in the strict sense of the word. What is needed most of all is enjoyment. As long as this is present, you can do almost anything.

18 MONDAY   *Moon Age Day 14   Moon Sign Capricorn*

A competitive attitude is stimulated by the trends that exist around you now. Although you may not be quite as lucky as is sometimes the case, you make up for this fact with a combination of sheer determination and the odd small calculated gamble. All in all, you should enjoy today fully.

19 TUESDAY   *Moon Age Day 15   Moon Sign Capricorn*

You are certainly concerned with practical ideas and won't be held back simply because others think you should be. So way out are some of your ideas and schemes at present that at least one person could accuse you of being mad. Never mind, it takes a sort of temporary insanity for genius to surface properly.

20 WEDNESDAY   *Moon Age Day 16   Moon Sign Capricorn*

The impact of your personality cannot be underestimated at this time and you are clearly intent on getting your own way, even if this means being something of a bully. Of course, this will not be your intention because you are too kind for that. So, look carefully before you leap in any direction.

21 THURSDAY   *Moon Age Day 17   Moon Sign Aquarius*

You have your work cut out with minor duties in and around your home. You have the chance to get on top of little jobs that have been piling up but you do need to take some time out to rest. Give yourself an hour or so to unwind, especially in good company, and allow others to be supportive.

22 FRIDAY   *Moon Age Day 18   Moon Sign Aquarius*

It would be sensible to keep life as simple as you can at the end of this working week. You won't help matters by biting off more than you can chew and will certainly gain greatly if you rely on the help and support that is on offer. In particular try to spend some time in the company of family members.

23 SATURDAY   *Moon Age Day 19   Moon Sign Pisces*

A few of your plans might be thrown into chaos, but take comfort from the fact that this is only for a few hours. The receding 'lunar low' can leave a feeling that you are not really in charge, but it is one you must dispel as quickly as possible. Routines help, and be aware that there is assistance around if you need it.

24 SUNDAY   *Moon Age Day 20   Moon Sign Pisces*

This is a day when you would welcome variety, but actually represents a period during which it is vital to ensure that you do the right thing at the correct moment. Balancing needs and desires is not going to be at all easy, but if you fail to do so, you will be the loser in the end.

25 MONDAY   *Moon Age Day 21   Moon Sign Aries*

You can keep on top of the game at work, though your approach is now more considered than will have been the case last week. People find you slightly more studious and certainly willing to listen to an alternative point of view. You are able to achieve much at present, mainly through hard work.

26 TUESDAY   *Moon Age Day 22   Moon Sign Aries*

If you wear a smile all day, things should work out better for you. The fact is that there is now plenty to smile about, if only because life appears so funny. Taking anything seriously is difficult and you even enjoy those jokes that are pointed in your direction. New friends may be about to come into your life.

27 WEDNESDAY   *Moon Age Day 23   Moon Sign Taurus*

Any nagging doubts about the direction your life has been taking ought to be fully dispelled now. You are totally in command and should be more than happy with your progress at work and possibly also in terms of romance. You won't want to take on too much in the way of new responsibility, at least for today.

28 THURSDAY   *Moon Age Day 24   Moon Sign Taurus*

Socially speaking, your powers of attraction are strong and you are inclined to seek out like-minded people at the moment. Don't be in the least surprised if more than one individual makes it clear that they find you attractive, and avoid being astonished when at least one of them points out the way they feel.

29 FRIDAY   *Moon Age Day 25   Moon Sign Gemini*

In your dealings with others, it is true that you could be slightly heavy-handed right now. It is important to remember that you need to show more tact and diplomacy than you expect those you deal with to show you. Saying it like it is might be fine, but to some people at least it can also be hurtful.

30 SATURDAY   *Moon Age Day 26   Moon Sign Gemini*

A very lucky phase is in operation at present, and it is one that looks set to stay with you into the working week. For now, don't worry too much about the details of life, but go with the flow and enjoy the challenges that are presented to you. It will be clear to everyone that you are exciting to have around.

31 SUNDAY   *Moon Age Day 27   Moon Sign Cancer*

Avoid run-ins with authority figures of any sort today and instead of addressing the practical aspects of life, concentrate instead on your social and romantic prospects. Spending time with family members is something that could appear particularly appealing now and as this is a summer weekend, short journeys might be good.

August 2016

1 MONDAY
Moon Age Day 28   Moon Sign Cancer

Although you are going to great lengths to please others today, in a significant number of cases this could be a waste of energy. It will seem as though some people are quite unwilling to co-operate, no matter how much effort you put in. Don't be annoyed, simply switch your efforts in a worthwhile direction instead.

2 TUESDAY
Moon Age Day 0   Moon Sign Cancer

The green light is on, at least it is in the early part of the day. Later you could find less support for your schemes and not everyone you expected to be on your team wants to play ball. Turn your attention in the direction of love because your popularity is still high in this area, and remains so for a while.

3 WEDNESDAY
Moon Age Day 1   Moon Sign Leo

In a holistic sense, this could probably turn out to be the very best day of the month. It isn't only the 'lunar high' that is working for you because a number of other planetary trends are also going your way. New ideas come into your mind all the time and your intuition is also particularly strong. You can afford to act on impulse.

4 THURSDAY
Moon Age Day 2   Moon Sign Leo

Have fun, that's what the stars are saying today. Most Leo people will be in a holiday frame of mind, even if it isn't actually possible to get away at present. Be bold and ambitious because this shows in your attitude and actions. In turn, such behaviour is likely to attract the support and the positive attention of others.

5 FRIDAY
Moon Age Day 3   Moon Sign Virgo

With a little gentle persuasion and the right attitude you can get more or less whatever you want from others today. This would be an ideal time for research of some sort, maybe in a library or on the internet. Communications of all sorts are especially rewarding and bring some slight changes in your own attitude.

6 SATURDAY
Moon Age Day 4   Moon Sign Virgo

You should be feeling good about family matters today. Something from the past could be replaying itself positively in your life at the moment, which may also put you in good spirits. Although there are few hours in which you can simply have fun, the practical side of life appeals to you and may prove to be reward enough in itself.

7 SUNDAY
Moon Age Day 5   Moon Sign Libra

Practical duties might turn out to be something of a bind today. If this turns out to be the case, leave them alone. This is Sunday after all. Spend some time daydreaming and thinking up new ideas that will be useful once another working week begins. At the same time, be prepared to put some energy into your social life.

8 MONDAY
Moon Age Day 6   Moon Sign Libra

You are still in a very optimistic frame of mind and can milk the situation for all you are worth. There could be financial gains to be made at the beginning of this week and you may be making great headway in career matters. Don't be too pushy in social settings and allow situations to mature in their own time.

9 TUESDAY
Moon Age Day 7   Moon Sign Libra

A sense of personal security might have you looking around your home and wondering how you can better protect what you have. That's fine, just as long as you do not become paranoid about the situation. Stay away from practical new starts, not because of the possibility of failure but to spend more time with those you love.

10 WEDNESDAY *Moon Age Day 8   Moon Sign Scorpio*

Most of your energy will probably be piled into your work, though if you are not working you won't find it hard to fill your hours. Much of what you do is on behalf of others and almost all your tasks today will carry a special sort of satisfaction. Don't be surprised if people are saying nice things about you.

11 THURSDAY *Moon Age Day 9   Moon Sign Scorpio*

You have the chance to make improvements of all kinds today. At work you may be sweeping up the dust of past happenings and looking forward with a new attitude. You can expect many changes in your life thanks to the present planetary positions and in particular that of your ruling planet, the Sun.

12 FRIDAY *Moon Age Day 10   Moon Sign Sagittarius*

Trips down memory lane represent at least one type of journey you will be taking right now. Although there isn't much future in the past for most Leo types, you do have moments when you look back and see life with a golden glow. There's no harm in this as a temporary interlude, but don't forget about progress too.

13 SATURDAY *Moon Age Day 11   Moon Sign Sagittarius*

This is a good time for romance and a weekend that offers a number of wonderful incentives. Avoid being anxious about issues that really do not matter and concentrate on having fun. A long walk might be enjoyable, or, if the more materialistic side of your nature is on display, a lengthy visit to the shops.

14 SUNDAY *Moon Age Day 12   Moon Sign Sagittarius*

You can't afford to take anything for granted now. Check and double check. If you do then the path to personal success should become far less rocky. It could be necessary to advertise your personal skills to the world at large because the right sort of people won't trip over you of their own accord.

15 MONDAY *Moon Age Day 13   Moon Sign Capricorn*

Changes are now inevitable, and you will want to revitalise aspects of your professional life that have not been working especially well recently. You might be surprised by the way particular people are treating you, probably because they are developing a new respect for your acumen.

16 TUESDAY *Moon Age Day 14   Moon Sign Capricorn*

Once again, you find yourself on the move and anxious to make the most of every moment during which you can put forward newer and more dynamic strategies. Romance is there for the taking and you might want to start by thinking up some compliments that nobody could ignore.

17 WEDNESDAY *Moon Age Day 15   Moon Sign Aquarius*

Instant success will not be coming your way today. The 'lunar low' holds back situations and makes it rather difficult for you to make the sort of progress you might wish. Use this as a contemplative period and a time when it is better to look ahead and plan, rather than to push forward in a direct sense.

18 THURSDAY *Moon Age Day 16   Moon Sign Aquarius*

You should keep your life as free from complications as proves to be possible at present. The 'lunar low' is still around and though it does little to depress you, it would be strange if you failed to notice that the going is somewhat tougher for the moment. Rely on close, personal attachments because these suit you the best now.

19 FRIDAY *Moon Age Day 17   Moon Sign Pisces*

There could be unexpected changes now in the offing, probably as a result of things you did some time ago. With a need to replay certain experiences and this time get them absolutely right, you can expect a degree of nostalgia to creep in too. A special friend is likely to seek you out soon.

20 SATURDAY   *Moon Age Day 18   Moon Sign Pisces*

Your ability to attract just the right sort of person stands you in good stead at the moment. Avoid listening too much to gossip and rumours, sticking only to the sort of facts that you can check out personally. Money matters should be steady and this is not the time for reckless gambles.

21 SUNDAY   *Moon Age Day 19   Moon Sign Aries*

Although this day is less satisfying in terms of overall success, you can get what you want in less obvious ways. Some people might call your present behaviour a little sneaky, but that is probably because they didn't think up your strategy first. Bear in mind that it is possible to score successes by using psychology instead of force.

22 MONDAY   *Moon Age Day 20   Moon Sign Aries*

You will have to keep a closer eye on your budget now because you are inclined to squander money at the very time you need it the most. An investment in travel could pay handsome dividends, if only in terms of your pleasure. With the working week ahead, you may decide the time is right to change location.

23 TUESDAY   *Moon Age Day 21   Moon Sign Taurus*

There might be a downside to matters associated with love. Affairs of the heart are not the best supported aspect of life today, thanks to the bearing Venus presently has on your life. Perhaps you don't fully understand what your partner is trying to say to you, or else their attitude is one that proves a mystery at the moment.

24 WEDNESDAY   *Moon Age Day 22   Moon Sign Taurus*

There are many comings and goings, leading to some confusion and uncertainty in specific areas of your life. This is likely to go against the grain and you will probably do everything you can to bring more discipline into your life. In discussions, look for the positive over the negative at all times.

25 THURSDAY *Moon Age Day 23   Moon Sign Gemini*

This ought to be a stable and productive time, particularly in terms of your personal life. It is now much easier to show the people you love that you are sincere and working towards their best interests. Insincerity is not part of your agenda, and now it is possible to prove this fact.

26 FRIDAY *Moon Age Day 24   Moon Sign Gemini*

You could feel yourself to be completely at the behest of other people today, possibly because of family commitments and obligations. It only takes small alterations in the way you are thinking in order to realise that you are the one in charge. Nothing really changes, but it does make you feel a good deal better.

27 SATURDAY *Moon Age Day 25   Moon Sign Gemini*

It is towards the domestic side of life that your mind is apt to turn at the present time. The weekend finds you paying specific attention to details in and around your home, but the fact that August is traditionally a month of greater freedom and movement might also mean your mind is geared towards thoughts of holidays.

28 SUNDAY *Moon Age Day 26   Moon Sign Cancer*

Leo is the sort of zodiac sign that occasionally fires from the hip and then regrets its untimely outbursts. If this has been the case for you recently, there is nothing at all wrong with apologising for your reaction, without having to admit you were wrong in substance. Humility is part of what you need today in order to prosper.

29 MONDAY *Moon Age Day 27   Moon Sign Cancer*

Financial consolidation and security are highlighted at the beginning of a new working week. Right now, you are a better saver than spender because thoughts of long-term security are on your mind. Maybe you are adopting a slightly modified mind set, which you may have to accept that not everyone is going to understand.

30 TUESDAY
Moon Age Day 28   Moon Sign Leo

Take all the ideas that have been sloshing about in your head and put them into practice today. Enjoy the fact that others find you difficult to miss and keep talking. Singing your own praises could be tedious, if it were not for the fact that you manage to do so in such a charming and entertaining way now. The 'lunar high' is on hand to help.

31 WEDNESDAY ☿
Moon Age Day 29   Moon Sign Leo

Putting just a little faith in Lady Luck is not a problem whilst the 'lunar high' stays around. You need to feel fulfilled today and to be sure that you are heading in your own chosen direction. If this isn't the case, you will soon become discontented. Only the most extreme form of activity will please you completely at the moment.

September 2016

1 THURSDAY ☿ Moon Age Day 0 Moon Sign Virgo

There could be a few mistakes made today as a result of simple oversights on your part. That is why it is necessary to work slowly and steadily towards your objectives, without rushing or pushing. There is assistance around if you are willing to look for it, though being a Leo subject you probably will not.

2 FRIDAY ☿ Moon Age Day 1 Moon Sign Virgo

It is towards work and practical matters that your mind is inclined to turn now. Routines can be rather boring because you want to break down fences and move forward progressively all the time. This isn't always possible and it is much more advisable on occasion to consolidate your position and to show patience.

3 SATURDAY ☿ Moon Age Day 2 Moon Sign Virgo

A little extra charm coming from your direction could go a long way in relationships this Saturday. Not only can you make others happy, but you are able to feather your own nest somewhat on the way. A partnership of some sort is getting stronger and results come in regarding efforts you have put in recently.

4 SUNDAY ☿ Moon Age Day 3 Moon Sign Libra

It is possible that you find circumstances conspiring to allow you a greater degree of personal freedom and self-choice. Grab the moment with both hands, despite the fact that this is Sunday. Even a very slight amount of pressure could convince others that your point of view is both measured and sensible today.

5 MONDAY ☿ *Moon Age Day 4   Moon Sign Libra*

Although you could find yourself feeling rather restless at the moment, this is a state of affairs that you can counter with a little imagination. Enrol friends in some of your latest enterprises, get out and about when you are not at work, and do your best to cheer everyone up. That should give you plenty to do.

6 TUESDAY ☿ *Moon Age Day 5   Moon Sign Scorpio*

There is help coming from above today. No, you don't need to look to angelic help from some passing cloud because it is superiors and people in positions of influence who may offer you their support. Try not to get too involved in the arguments or discussions of other people. They can only cloud your horizons now.

7 WEDNESDAY ☿ *Moon Age Day 6   Moon Sign Scorpio*

A wonderfully romantic interlude is on the way. Those Leo subjects who are not directly looking for love could find they are on the receiving end of affection in any case. Try not to do more than you have to early in the day, but by the time the late afternoon and evening come along you are raring to get up and go.

8 THURSDAY ☿ *Moon Age Day 7   Moon Sign Scorpio*

The peace and quiet you may desire at home today probably won't be forthcoming. People want to visit you and may bring other friends with them. All in all, it could turn out to be an active sort of day. On the one hand you might moan about this, but being a Leo subject you should be pleased that life is eventful.

9 FRIDAY ☿ *Moon Age Day 8   Moon Sign Sagittarius*

Out there in the practical world, you are likely to finish the working week with a definite flourish. Once responsibility is out of the way you should be in the mood to have fun. Incidents that happen today could well send your mind spinning into the past. However, you won't find much that is of use to you in that country.

10 SATURDAY ☿ *Moon Age Day 9* *Moon Sign Sagittarius*

It is possible that today may bring the odd monetary setback. In a way it doesn't really matter because the most important things in life now come to you free of charge. You can't put a value on the love of family members or the friendship of pals who seem determined to put themselves out on your behalf.

11 SUNDAY ☿ *Moon Age Day 10* *Moon Sign Capricorn*

For the young or young-at-heart Leo the romantic possibilities of today are pronounced. It isn't so much what you feel for others that counts right now, more the way you are able to put it into words. At work, you have been steaming ahead recently. Now it's time to play and Leo manages that wonderfully.

12 MONDAY ☿ *Moon Age Day 11* *Moon Sign Capricorn*

Romantic matters continue to be positively highlighted at this time. This stage of September can sometimes be very pleasant in terms of weather and this would be an ideal time to take your lover on a little trip somewhere. It is probably in the evening that the most intimate contacts are likely, with a busier daytime period.

13 TUESDAY ☿ *Moon Age Day 12* *Moon Sign Aquarius*

Your powers of vitality are taking something of a dive today. Because you have been galloping along so fast, the sudden brake applied by the 'lunar low' is that much more noticeable. Don't be disheartened. Simply sit back and mull things over for a day or two. Everyone needs a rest, even irrepressible Leo.

14 WEDNESDAY ☿ *Moon Age Day 13* *Moon Sign Aquarius*

It might be sensible to put at least a few of your ideas on hold. Instead of dealing with the practicalities of life, spend some time with people you find interesting, and who have a positive view of you. Your ego needs massaging and what you definitely don't require at the moment are comments that belittle you in any way.

15 THURSDAY ☿ *Moon Age Day 14   Moon Sign Aquarius*

Don't risk overturning recent successes by being impatient or expecting too much of yourself. A slow and steady sort of Thursday is on offer, which turns out to be no bad thing. Socialise when you can and turn your mind once again to showing your loved ones how important they are to you. Emotions are close to the surface.

16 FRIDAY ☿ *Moon Age Day 15   Moon Sign Pisces*

Your co-operative spirit is strong and you can get along just fine now by combining your own powers with those of the people you like the most. If there are any individuals around at present who do not care for you, simply shrug your shoulders and accept the fact that you cannot be universally popular.

17 SATURDAY ☿ *Moon Age Day 16   Moon Sign Pisces*

When it comes to talking to colleagues today, you stand a chance of getting a very sympathetic ear and even offers of practical assistance. People you haven't seen for ages are likely to come back into your life any time now, and may bring with them some heartening and even amusing news.

18 SUNDAY ☿ *Moon Age Day 17   Moon Sign Aries*

This is definitely the very best time to impress someone important. Although the chance of making a professional splash is somewhat diminished at the weekend the social possibilities are potentially wonderful. Don't let the grass grow under your feet and be willing to go out and get what you want.

19 MONDAY ☿ *Moon Age Day 18   Moon Sign Aries*

Enjoying the social mainstream, you embark upon a new week with vigour, and the sort of sense of humour that might be described as robust. When it comes to getting what you want, you are hardly likely to take no for an answer at this time and will be quite pleased with some of your little successes.

20 TUESDAY ☿ *Moon Age Day 19* *Moon Sign Taurus*

Remain open to new input and don't close your mind to anything, just because it sounds odd at first. You need to improve your credibility now and to show those around you how keen you are to get on in life. It appears that someone quite important has been watching you, and they are likely to let you know it before long.

21 WEDNESDAY ☿ *Moon Age Day 20* *Moon Sign Taurus*

There may be a few unexpected demands being made of you now, and that could mean having to be rather more flexible than has been the case during the last few days. This is particularly true in the case of relatives, or friends who are having problems. Write a letter or an email to someone you really miss at present.

22 THURSDAY *Moon Age Day 21* *Moon Sign Gemini*

There are some issues that seem to be a real chore today, and the sadness is that there is no getting away from them. Better by far to pitch in early and to get such jobs out of the way. Later on, you can begin to have some real fun, doing things that have a constant and lasting appeal.

23 FRIDAY *Moon Age Day 22* *Moon Sign Gemini*

It is unlikely that your home life could be called boring at present. People demand your time and your advice and there is likely to be lots of coming and going. Things could be somewhat quieter at work, however, and you may feel that a little extra incentive is required before long.

24 SATURDAY *Moon Age Day 23* *Moon Sign Cancer*

Not all communications are going well today, probably because there are people around who simply don't want to listen to what you would call reason. It might be best to drop contentious issues for a day or two and to concentrate more on issues on which everyone in your circle can agree.

25 SUNDAY
Moon Age Day 24   Moon Sign Cancer

Certain plans remain on hold, though that doesn't mean you are having a boring time. On the contrary, if you stick to personal ideals and enlist the support of family members, you can still have a happy and a productive day. The more practical issues of life need another day before you pitch in again with gusto.

26 MONDAY
Moon Age Day 25   Moon Sign Leo

Fresh starts are on the way and the 'lunar high' offers you the best incentive this month to get stuck in and have a go. This would be a great day for travel, or for putting across to other people some of your most treasured ideas. Your razor sharp wit will help you to avoid unnecessary confrontation.

27 TUESDAY
Moon Age Day 26   Moon Sign Leo

A physical and mental peak arrives for many sons and daughters of the Sun. Keep up the pressure and let people know what you want from life. There are many occasions today when even strangers would lend a hand if they only knew what it was you are after. Finances should strengthen, though you are spending wisely at present.

28 WEDNESDAY
Moon Age Day 27   Moon Sign Virgo

Nostalgic pursuits of one sort or another could be highly rewarding today. For example, you might decide to take a trip that will bring back personal memories, or simply discuss the past with friends. The accent today should be on your social life, rather than on practical issues as a whole.

29 THURSDAY
Moon Age Day 28   Moon Sign Virgo

It could be that you are putting your point of view across in a way that others would see as being contentious. Be careful that you do not offer offence, even unintentionally. Trying to be tactful all the time won't be easy, but it can pay quite definite dividends, both personally and perhaps even financially.

30 FRIDAY
Moon Age Day 0   Moon Sign Virgo

Professional issues can be complicated today and need careful handling. However, don't allow them to spill over into your personal and social life, which also demand more of your time at present. Consider the needs of friends today and involve them in your plans, particularly someone who is down in the dumps.

October

2016

1 SATURDAY
Moon Age Day 1   Moon Sign Libra

Look out for minor conflict with others, particularly in group situations. The fact is that you often want to be top dog, and even when you don't mind, others think that you belong at the head of things. Resolving such difficulties will take patience and tact – though you will still end up running the show.

2 SUNDAY
Moon Age Day 2   Moon Sign Libra

Minor tensions could be in evidence, particularly at home. You may decide it is better to spend more time with friends right now, taking the heat off domestic situations. If you are at work you should be active and genuinely taking a role when it proves to be most important to do so.

3 MONDAY
Moon Age Day 3   Moon Sign Scorpio

The creative side of your nature is very much emphasised by prevailing planetary trends. Perhaps you are deciding to make changes in and around your home and if so you should consult your partner. Other family members also have their part to play and it really is a case of being open to opinion now.

4 TUESDAY
Moon Age Day 4   Moon Sign Scorpio

For the first part of the day you will be taking things steadily, but once you get the bit between your teeth, it's onward and upward once more. Keep an open mind about the attitudes and opinions of a friend, which may sound radical and even quite bonkers. They may simply be going through a tricky period.

5 WEDNESDAY   *Moon Age Day 5   Moon Sign Scorpio*

New and enlivening experiences are just around the next corner. You may become a little frustrated that they don't turn up immediately, but that's the nature of Leo. Stay cool, calm and collected, even when you feel yourself provoked. If you do so there is a good chance you will win through any obstacle.

6 THURSDAY   *Moon Age Day 6   Moon Sign Sagittarius*

Socially speaking there are plenty of light-hearted and enjoyable moments today. Look out for new people coming into your life. They might not signify too much at the moment but it is only a matter of time before these same individuals begin to play a much more important part in your plans for the future.

7 FRIDAY   *Moon Age Day 7   Moon Sign Sagittarius*

Don't be too obsessed with having everything perfectly organised today. A little disorganisation may even prove to be a blessing in disguise. Confidence is still present, though seems to take a holiday when you are faced with a brand new challenge of a sort that hasn't come your way before.

8 SATURDAY   *Moon Age Day 8   Moon Sign Capricorn*

With the weekend comes a chance to enlist the help and co-operation of other people. It was inevitable right at the start of October that you would vacillate between listening and acting on impulse but today finds you very compliant. Saturday ought to offer good social prospects and a chance for new enterprises.

9 SUNDAY   *Moon Age Day 9   Moon Sign Capricorn*

Sunday brings relief from something that has been nagging at you for a while. Circumstances may force you down slower paths but a little circumspection won't do you any harm at all. Look ahead towards the coming week and work now towards special social functions that have been planned for a while.

10 MONDAY   *Moon Age Day 10   Moon Sign Capricorn*

You are your own best public relations officer today – frank, fearless and bold, yet at the same time caring and willing to listen. These really are the very best qualities of your zodiac sign and they are obvious for all to see. As a result you ought to find yourself on the receiving end of a very happy day.

11 TUESDAY   *Moon Age Day 11   Moon Sign Aquarius*

The information you receive from other people turns out to be both interesting and potentially helpful. For this reason alone it is worth keeping your ears open. Even gossip does not fall beneath your contempt for once, though of course being a Leo subject you certainly won't believe everything you hear.

12 WEDNESDAY   *Moon Age Day 12   Moon Sign Aquarius*

The planets offer little assistance to your plans for today, though you probably did manage to get at least half way through the 'lunar low' without realising it was present. It would be best to keep a low profile for the moment, allowing other people to take some of the strain and being willing to accept intervention and advice.

13 THURSDAY   *Moon Age Day 13   Moon Sign Pisces*

Don't make life any more difficult than it needs to be by chasing up every detail or insisting on having your say. There are times now when it would definitely be best to keep quiet, rather than to cause problems for yourself. This stage of the working week could easily be marred with disputes, so take care to avoid them.

14 FRIDAY   *Moon Age Day 14   Moon Sign Pisces*

Relationships tend to be rewarding today, which is why you may decide to drop most responsibilities and practical issues in favour of having fun. There are people around who make you laugh, and who are just as fond of you as you are of them. This is definitely not a day during which you need to complicate anything.

15 SATURDAY
Moon Age Day 15   Moon Sign Aries

There are ways and means to increase your income at this time, though you have to dig hard within your own reserves to put them into practice. You won't be tardy when it comes to putting your ideas across, especially when you are in the company of people who already think you are well on the way to being a genius.

16 SUNDAY
Moon Age Day 16   Moon Sign Aries

Monetary decisions made now should turn out to be highly profitable. Not everyone is willing to support you however, and you could have trouble with certain acquaintances. In terms of plain friendship, you will find the people who have been around the longest are the ones you want to rely on.

17 MONDAY
Moon Age Day 17   Moon Sign Taurus

Career developments are helped by your capacity for hard work and your determination, which could be said to be legendary at the moment. You may still have to cope with a number of distractions that will thwart some of your intentions and test your patience once again. Friendships are very tight and secure today.

18 TUESDAY
Moon Age Day 18   Moon Sign Taurus

Certain communication issues can be marred by disagreements, which is a pity at a time when you are getting on famously with almost everyone. Convincing colleagues that your ideas are better than theirs won't be easy, but is necessary all the same. By the evening you will simply want to have a good time.

19 WEDNESDAY
Moon Age Day 19   Moon Sign Gemini

It seems that new technology has a particular fascination for you around now. Whether you are acquiring a new mobile phone, or getting to grips with computer software, you are turning your various skills in new directions and enjoying the cut and thrust of a generally busy life.

20 THURSDAY *Moon Age Day 20   Moon Sign Gemini*

Financially speaking, you seem to be on a winning streak, so you can afford to push your luck a little more than usual. This is another of those days that responds best to a light touch and to a change of scene if possible. The everyday routines of a normal working Thursday don't hold much attraction for you right now.

21 FRIDAY *Moon Age Day 21   Moon Sign Cancer*

You can get most of what you want today by using a little gentle persuasion. There are people around who show genuine and sincere resistance to some of your ideas, which is why you have to turn on the charm and explain your point of view rationally and fairly. Your partner might need extra support now.

22 SATURDAY *Moon Age Day 22   Moon Sign Cancer*

The focus today appears to be on personal relationships. With everything to play for in the emotional stakes, and the weekend offering a good deal of incentive, you need to show those around you, and particularly your romantic partner, how much they mean to you. Social highlights abound.

23 SUNDAY *Moon Age Day 23   Moon Sign Leo*

It's up and away now as the 'lunar high' comes along, allowing you to live life to the full. You may find it possible to solve a problem that has been dogging you for quite some time and it ought to be quite clear that you enjoy great popularity now. Financially speaking you could find a boost coming your way.

24 MONDAY *Moon Age Day 24   Moon Sign Leo*

This could be a superb time for putting new ideas into practice. Don't be held back by negative types and once you have made up your mind to go in any given direction, keep moving. Your social life should be a breeze and with more and more popularity coming your way there are new people joining the fan club.

25 TUESDAY
Moon Age Day 25   Moon Sign Leo

There is a strong emphasis on material pleasures and life supplies you with the means to enjoy them. It is possible that efforts you have put in previously now begin to bear fruit and at the same time, you are still working hard towards your ultimate objectives. There ought to be some hours to spoil yourself today.

26 WEDNESDAY
Moon Age Day 26   Moon Sign Virgo

You benefit today from time spent at home, and amongst family members. The bright lights of the social world probably won't mean as much for the moment and simple pleasures tend to predominate. This would be an ideal interlude to treat the middle of the week like a weekend because you probably won't feel much like work.

27 THURSDAY
Moon Age Day 27   Moon Sign Virgo

Some aspects of your daily life could simply be breaking down or going wrong right now. Don't panic. This is a temporary phase and in any case there will still be enough positive action to keep you amused and entertained. Not everyone seems to be on your side right now, which itself could be a small problem.

28 FRIDAY
Moon Age Day 28   Moon Sign Libra

The brisk pace of life continues around you, though whether or not you are taking much part in it remains to be seen. It's almost as if the world and its happenings is a river that you are watching flow by. Standing there on the bank you get a very different perspective, and it's one that could be quite informative.

29 SATURDAY
Moon Age Day 29   Moon Sign Libra

Things change overnight and there is rarely a dull moment now. Although you have some home-loving tendencies at present, it appears that you are willing to take your nearest and dearest with you on a flight of fancy. Transposing some of your dreams into reality might be hard, but that doesn't mean you should abandon the effort.

30 SUNDAY
Moon Age Day 0   Moon Sign Libra

The intellectual peak is still around for the moment. The present position of the Sun causes you to display a mentally alert and quite inspirational nature to the world at large. Answers to potential problems come thick and fast, one or two of them from the least likely directions before the end of the day.

31 MONDAY
Moon Age Day 1   Moon Sign Scorpio

The start of the new working week brings a great boost to all matters practical and professional. You will be looking and feeling especially good now and are able to enjoy yourself in almost any company. Routines really won't appeal because you are too full of bounce and want to do so many different things.

November 2016

1 TUESDAY
Moon Age Day 2   Moon Sign Scorpio

A new month but it's business as usual as far as you are concerned. With plenty to keep you occupied, you look forward positively. The approach of winter might not be too appealing to you now, but you have the chance to create a warm atmosphere in the next couple of months, no matter what the weather is doing.

2 WEDNESDAY
Moon Age Day 3   Moon Sign Sagittarius

Family issues may arise which will need your attention today. Your confidence remains high in personal situations but may be less obvious in practical matters. This may not be the most productive part of the week, particularly in a financial sense. Simply move forward steadily and don't allow your plans to be diverted.

3 THURSDAY
Moon Age Day 4   Moon Sign Sagittarius

Your ego is boosted when you are at the forefront of situations and you won't take kindly to being put at the back of any queue right now. Try to stay calm, even if you feel you are under personal pressure and certainly do not defend yourself when it is obvious to almost everyone that you are not under attack.

4 FRIDAY
Moon Age Day 5   Moon Sign Sagittarius

Social and romantic issues ought to prove quite satisfying, probably making for an interesting and even a special sort of Friday. You should enjoy a feeling of personal contentment and you are now less likely to overreact to minor issues than might have been the case earlier in the week.

5 SATURDAY
Moon Age Day 6   Moon Sign Capricorn

Not everything on your agenda can be dealt with as quickly or efficiently as you might wish. This means showing patience and also being willing to allow other people to lend a hand. It might be the case that you have been holding specific individuals back, simply because you will not relinquish control.

6 SUNDAY
Moon Age Day 7   Moon Sign Capricorn

A boost to optimism and your overall sense of freedom is evident now. You want to explore new avenues and the present position of Mercury improves your ability to communicate positively. You may find yourself getting on well with people who have not figured in your life at all previously.

7 MONDAY
Moon Age Day 8   Moon Sign Aquarius

There are some limitations to be faced today and tomorrow. This is more or less entirely due to the 'lunar low' and there probably isn't very much you can do about it. Instead of bemoaning the fact, enjoy some rest and relaxation. There is no obstacle in the way of fun, especially when this is of a low-key type.

8 TUESDAY
Moon Age Day 9   Moon Sign Aquarius

Don't take any big risks today. Be willing to settle for a peaceful life and allow others to take the strain. You are undergoing a sea-change in thinking at the moment and this does not allow you the time and space for moments of reflection. In reality, you should get a good deal more done right now than you expect.

9 WEDNESDAY
Moon Age Day 10   Moon Sign Pisces

You could do far worse today than taking off into the wide blue yonder. With a restless streak on display, you will not want to be tied down to too many routines, though you are not in a solitary mood and will respond to company. Try not to react too harshly if you feel you are under interrogation.

10 THURSDAY   *Moon Age Day 11   Moon Sign Pisces*

Some of the personal changes that are going on in your life at the moment need looking at very carefully. It is possible that you are being forced down paths you don't really want to follow. Friends will be on your side in minor disputes but it would be better to avoid these altogether if possible.

11 FRIDAY   *Moon Age Day 12   Moon Sign Pisces*

Career matters seem to be a test of patience today but your responsibility to work is unlikely to extend into the evening. Whatever time you have to call your own, spend it in the company of people who interest you. Do a little questioning if you want to get to the bottom of a specific issue.

12 SATURDAY   *Moon Age Day 13   Moon Sign Aries*

It looks as though there are now specific, important changes taking place in your life. These are likely to have a bearing on personal aspects of your day and might involve a shift in emphasis with regard to relationships. Some interesting people will be crossing your path around now and they can all teach you something.

13 SUNDAY   *Moon Age Day 14   Moon Sign Aries*

This should be a lovely time for all intimate matters. Quite a few planetary indicators are suggesting that love is in the air, together with friendship and a feeling of togetherness. The hard edge of Leo certainly isn't on display at this time and it is likely that certain people will realise what an old softy you really are.

14 MONDAY   *Moon Age Day 15   Moon Sign Taurus*

All of a sudden it is possible that you will find yourself on what seems like an emotional roller-coaster. Trying to come to terms with exactly what others expect of you isn't going to be easy, unless you are psychic, of course! Take the simplest route to get yourself in the know and ask someone's advice.

15 TUESDAY *Moon Age Day 16   Moon Sign Taurus*

Minor disagreements, particularly at home, are really not necessary. Instead of falling out, talk things through calmly and rationally. Friends should be co-operative and anxious to have you with them when the good times roll. Although you might be quite tired today, there is a good chance you will join in.

16 WEDNESDAY *Moon Age Day 17   Moon Sign Gemini*

You won't want to believe everything you hear today, though be cautious, because at least some of it will be true. Confidence is growing all the time in a professional sense, but you can be too clever for your own good. It is important to check and recheck all facts and figures before proceeding with any specific deal.

17 THURSDAY *Moon Age Day 18   Moon Sign Gemini*

Get an early start with all important projects and ideas. The more you get done in the morning, the greater the amount of time you will have to please yourself later. It might be difficult to prevent yourself from doing tasks that rightfully belong in the middle of next week, but that's just the way you are feeling now.

18 FRIDAY *Moon Age Day 19   Moon Sign Cancer*

This could be a good time for information gathering and for playing the Sherlock Holmes. You are curious about almost everything and anxious to get to the bottom of puzzles that have bugged you for quite some time. Routines are not particularly appealing, though better if you have the chance to share them.

19 SATURDAY *Moon Age Day 20   Moon Sign Cancer*

All of a sudden, you find yourself in a very contemplative phase, but you should be able to indulge this if you have worked hard during the week. You can't afford to risk your happiness at the moment, and, deep inside, you know it. Keep it straight and level today, but don't worry about matters you cannot alter.

20 SUNDAY
Moon Age Day 21   Moon Sign Leo

Press ahead with all major plans and don't allow yourself to be held back when you can see that the going is good. There ought to be plenty to occupy your mind and your body today, with the start of a new working week in view which is likely bring forth new possibilities of both a professional and a personal nature.

21 MONDAY
Moon Age Day 22   Moon Sign Leo

This would be a good time to put your luck to the test. Although you won't want to put your shirt on the next horse running, you may wish to take a small calculated financial risk. The planets suggest better than average expectations of success. Prudence should be your watch-word though, and you should not act without careful consideration.

22 TUESDAY
Moon Age Day 23   Moon Sign Virgo

Career-wise, this is likely to be a very steady time, with not much to recommend it. Because of this, you need to turn your attention in other directions, with love playing an important part in your thinking. Avoid tactless approaches and make sure you practice what you are going to say in important meetings.

23 WEDNESDAY
Moon Age Day 24   Moon Sign Virgo

The further you can reach, the better you feel today. That doesn't mean you should knock yourself out, which isn't exactly the right recipe for success in the longer-term. You need pace and a good deal of common sense if you want to make the most of every opportunity, of which there are many now.

24 THURSDAY
Moon Age Day 25   Moon Sign Libra

Your domestic life may be dogged by disagreements or disputes of a totally unnecessary kind. Try to avoid these by staying cool and by keeping your funny head on whenever possible. Your creative potential is good and you might decide to brighten up your home in a number of different ways.

25 FRIDAY
Moon Age Day 26   Moon Sign Libra

You should carry on seeking the new and unusual in life at every opportunity today. Don't be too tied up with details and make certain that you associate at some stage today with people you genuinely find interesting. Even if you are feeling very slightly out of sorts with yourself, you can enjoy the day.

26 SATURDAY
Moon Age Day 27   Moon Sign Libra

The Sun has now entered your solar fifth house, bringing a time when it is quite possible to let your light shine. The necessary balance between confidence and arrogance is achieved wonderfully in your case – particularly so today. It isn't likely that anyone would doubt you at the moment.

27 SUNDAY
Moon Age Day 28   Moon Sign Scorpio

Making concessions to others should now come easily and co-operative ventures can prove to be both lucrative and very interesting. Stretching your imagination isn't hard right now and it appears that as a storyteller you are second to none. This should certainly impress younger family members or the children of friends.

28 MONDAY
Moon Age Day 29   Moon Sign Scorpio

Whatever helps you enjoy your life the most, that's what you are looking for on this Monday. Somewhat less settled than yesterday, but also more inspirational, you are unlikely to opt for second best. You need to be with people who are as keen as you are to have fun, sometimes in quite surprising ways.

29 TUESDAY
Moon Age Day 0   Moon Sign Sagittarius

Your sense of personal security is boosted by trends and events today. This would be a good time to involve yourself in DIY projects, or for supervising someone else to do work in and around your home. Secretly, though, in the inner recesses of your mind you are seeking long-term stability.

30 WEDNESDAY *Moon Age Day 1 Moon Sign Sagittarius*

Your powers of attraction are in the ascendant and you would rarely find a better day than this for getting on side with someone you have fancied for a while. If this merely represents a fantasy there is probably no harm done. Don't be too quick to judge a friend who has acted rashly.

December
2016

1 THURSDAY
Moon Age Day 2   Moon Sign Sagittarius

It is important to go with the flow today. There are potential gains coming your way from a number of different directions and as you already have your social head on, the run-up to Christmas probably begins here for you. Concentrate on specific tasks that could prove awkward if you lose sight of the major objectives.

2 FRIDAY
Moon Age Day 3   Moon Sign Capricorn

Although you could find there are one or two professional setbacks to be addressed, in the main you are progressive, hopeful and aspirational. Turn your mind away from work later in the day, towards fun and games, which become an increasing part of your life as the month advances. Your confidence remains solid.

3 SATURDAY
Moon Age Day 4   Moon Sign Capricorn

There are others to contend with today, one or two of whom are anxious for you to follow their lead. To do so probably won't appeal and the difficulty lies in letting them know this fact, without inadvertently offering offence. A little mistake made early in the day should be easy to put right later.

4 SUNDAY
Moon Age Day 5   Moon Sign Aquarius

There are various tests of your patience at present and there isn't really very much you can do about them. The 'lunar low' holds you back and makes it difficult for you to show the stronger side of your nature that has predominated recently. Confidence is only a short time away, but it isn't present today or tomorrow.

5 MONDAY
Moon Age Day 6   Moon Sign Aquarius

If you can avoid doing too much work today then so much the better. The 'lunar low' makes you lethargic and much more willing than usual to put your feet up. Keep a low profile socially too, maybe settling for spending some hours on your own. At least the rest should do you good.

6 TUESDAY
Moon Age Day 7   Moon Sign Aquarius

You may be undergoing important personal changes and there is no doubt that the lethargic period brought about by the 'lunar low' is now left far behind. Be willing to commit yourself to new schemes and enterprises when you know they are going to prove positive in the longer-term. Friends should be helpful if you need them.

7 WEDNESDAY
Moon Age Day 8   Moon Sign Pisces

Along comes a brand new influence, increasing your desire for new experiences and causing you to willingly throw over traditions and routines. This is fine for you, but with Christmas not far away you have to respect the fact that some people close to you want to leave things the way they are.

8 THURSDAY
Moon Age Day 9   Moon Sign Pisces

Your best area at the moment comes through travel, intellectual stimulation of almost any sort and through simple human contact. Still friendly, and very anxious to help others, you seek out good causes and do whatever you can to get the rest of the world into the same optimistic state that you presently experience.

9 FRIDAY
Moon Age Day 10   Moon Sign Aries

Look out for small pressures coming from a number of different directions. Calm down an over-active nervous system and avoid allowing yourself to be become too fixated about any aspect of life. Cool and steady is what works for you best this Friday, and you are more than capable of adopting this state.

10 SATURDAY   *Moon Age Day 11   Moon Sign Aries*

This is a time to be seeking wide, open spaces. The weekend offers a sense of freedom and the chance to do something different. What you wouldn't take kindly to right now is being restricted in any way. There are plenty of people around you who would be only too pleased to join you on a flight of fancy.

11 SUNDAY   *Moon Age Day 12   Moon Sign Taurus*

Doing your own thing seems to you to be the key to happiness at the moment, although consider whether this is actually true. Take time out to join in some family madness and you will lighten any significant professional load. You may also be the best person to bolster the resolve of a friend who is trying to alter their life.

12 MONDAY   *Moon Age Day 13   Moon Sign Taurus*

Since work seems to be fairly progressive, and in the main looking after itself, you will probably be turning your attention to other matters. Your confidence remains generally high on the social scene, and you may decide to embark upon new interests that have been at the back of your mind for a while.

13 TUESDAY   *Moon Age Day 14   Moon Sign Gemini*

A loved one, or your romantic partner, will probably be expressing some rather strong opinions at present. Be creative in your responses and don't allow yourself to become unsettled by matters that you can deal with quite easily. There are some interesting opportunities to change aspects of your working life.

14 WEDNESDAY   *Moon Age Day 15   Moon Sign Gemini*

There is an emphasis today upon pleasure, and finding it wherever you can. Your commitment to the practical side of life is much less emphasised for a day or two, leaving you determined to please yourself in every other way. Accept that not everyone is going to understand your present attitude.

15 THURSDAY *Moon Age Day 16   Moon Sign Cancer*

You should find the time today to think about work, and the reasons why you might have been shying away from it since the weekend. If there is any one issue that troubles you, sort it out now. A slight sense of lethargy still prevails, but is unlikely to last long as a new breeze of opportunity begins to blow.

16 FRIDAY *Moon Age Day 17   Moon Sign Cancer*

There are a number of obligations around today that leave little time for you to concentrate on your own life. Since this is fairly typical of the sort of person you are, it probably will not worry you too much, if at all. Last-minute planning for Christmas is part of the recipe for an interesting period.

17 SATURDAY *Moon Age Day 18   Moon Sign Leo*

This is the best part of the month when it comes to having the necessary get up and go to really change your life and its circumstances. With a good deal of empathy, and a great desire to please others, there is no reason at all why you should ruffle any feathers. Life is hectic, but it should be settled too.

18 SUNDAY *Moon Age Day 19   Moon Sign Leo*

This is another day on which you should have plenty to say for yourself and no shortage of energy with which to get things done. Creature comforts are not very important to you at the moment and you are quite prepared to go through some discomfort in order to achieve your objectives. You are also extremely friendly today.

19 MONDAY *Moon Age Day 20   Moon Sign Virgo*

This could be one of the best days of the month to make new starts at work. Of course, you might find this difficult with Christmas immediately around the corner but you can start a few balls rolling and will probably be pleased to do so. Co-operation with co-workers can also be a key to success.

20 TUESDAY ☿ *Moon Age Day 21 Moon Sign Virgo*

Happily on the go today, you find the possibility of any sort of travel to be quite exciting. You are now less inclined to stay in one spot in any case and might be braving the crowds to do some important Christmas shopping. A general sense of goodwill seems to pervade your life now.

21 WEDNESDAY ☿ *Moon Age Day 22 Moon Sign Virgo*

A few small drawbacks at work are possible today, but these might be due to the fact that you find it difficult to keep your mind on the job at hand. In other ways, you are busy right now and possibly getting certain aspects of the festive season slightly out of proportion. Concentrate on the domestic scene.

22 THURSDAY ☿ *Moon Age Day 23 Moon Sign Libra*

Someone, somewhere, ought to be making you feel really good, simply by saying and doing the right things. You have plenty to occupy your mind right now, but you should spend at least a few moments looking around yourself today and working out where your priorities should be at this time of year.

23 FRIDAY ☿ *Moon Age Day 24 Moon Sign Libra*

Practical matters are likely to turn out the way you would wish. Last-minute planning and preparations should go well, but you could be slightly bothered by the attitude of friends, which may seem odd. Family members will be pestering you all the time, especially younger people, but this probably won't be a problem to you.

24 SATURDAY ☿ *Moon Age Day 25 Moon Sign Scorpio*

Look out for a Christmas Eve that finds you busy and very progressive in attitude. However, the important aspects of today could easily be romantic ones. Maybe it's the time of year, or perhaps your own attitude, but you should find that your partner is very much more responsive and inclined to say just the right things to you.

25 SUNDAY ☿ *Moon Age Day 26   Moon Sign Scorpio*

There is something distinctly weird and wonderful about this Christmas Day, though not in a difficult sense. Some unusual experiences are likely, together with messages from people you may not have been in contact with for ages. All in all, this is a day for good communications and for enjoying the antics of others.

26 MONDAY ☿ *Moon Age Day 27   Moon Sign Scorpio*

You can accomplish a great deal around now and won't have much difficulty finding people who want to go along with your ideas. Interrupting the flow of festivities, you now have your practical head on and may be turning your thoughts towards work, whether you are actually there or not.

27 TUESDAY ☿ *Moon Age Day 28   Moon Sign Sagittarius*

You can learn something new and exciting now. Keep your ears open and be willing to alter your plans at the last minute in order to achieve something splendid. It's turning out to be a hectic and effective period between Christmas and New Year but don't forget that part of the reason for holidays is to have a rest.

28 WEDNESDAY ☿ *Moon Age Day 29   Moon Sign Sagittarius*

What matters most today is feeling useful and being able to offer sound counsel to people who have problems of one sort or another. You are entering a very positive phase romantically speaking, and one that predominates until well after the holidays. Not everyone is being equally co-operative however.

29 THURSDAY ☿ *Moon Age Day 0   Moon Sign Capricorn*

A strong emphasis now shows on leisure and pleasure – probably not a moment too soon. In a practical sense you will simply have to be patient. There is nothing to be gained right now from rushing your fences and there are so few people at work this week some of your efforts would be wasted in any case.

30 FRIDAY ☿ *Moon Age Day 1   Moon Sign Capricorn*

Avoid being too extravagant today. There is a possibility that you are spending money you don't actually possess, and this could lead to a few worries that might extend some way into January. You need to be realistic, and to persuade those around you to take a similar attitude.

31 SATURDAY ☿ *Moon Age Day 2   Moon Sign Capricorn*

Your social life ought to prove quite rewarding on this New Year's Eve. Your creative potential is also good and you may have decided to make some sort of change at home. As long as it is something that makes you more comfortable, and not less so, then your efforts are worthwhile. Let someone else undertake a domestic task.

RISING SIGNS FOR LEO

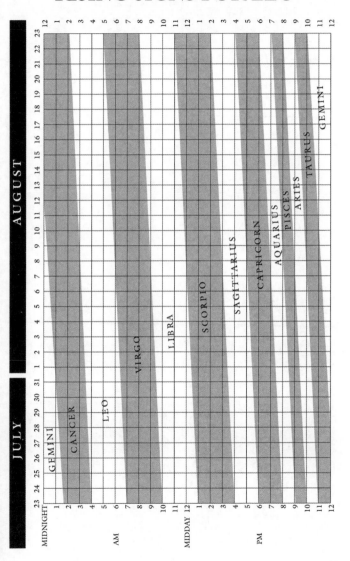

THE ZODIAC, PLANETS AND CORRESPONDENCES

The Earth revolves around the Sun once every calendar year, so when viewed from Earth the Sun appears in a different part of the sky as the year progresses. In astrology, these parts of the sky are divided into the signs of the zodiac and this means that the signs are organised in a circle. The circle begins with Aries and ends with Pisces.

Taking the zodiac sign as a starting point, astrologers then work with all the positions of planets, stars and many other factors to calculate horoscopes and birth charts and tell us what the stars have in store for us.

The table below shows the planets and Elements for each of the signs of the zodiac. Each sign belongs to one of the four Elements: Fire, Air, Earth or Water. Fire signs are creative and enthusiastic; Air signs are mentally active and thoughtful; Earth signs are constructive and practical; Water signs are emotional and have strong feelings.

It also shows the metals and gemstones associated with, or corresponding with, each sign. The correspondence is made when a metal or stone possesses properties that are held in common with a particular sign of the zodiac.

Finally, the table shows the opposite of each star sign – this is the opposite sign in the astrological circle.

Placed	Sign	Symbol	Element	Planet	Metal	Stone	Opposite
1	Aries	Ram	Fire	Mars	Iron	Bloodstone	Libra
2	Taurus	Bull	Earth	Venus	Copper	Sapphire	Scorpio
3	Gemini	Twins	Air	Mercury	Mercury	Tiger's Eye	Sagittarius
4	Cancer	Crab	Water	Moon	Silver	Pearl	Capricorn
5	Leo	Lion	Fire	Sun	Gold	Ruby	Aquarius
6	Virgo	Maiden	Earth	Mercury	Mercury	Sardonyx	Pisces
7	Libra	Scales	Air	Venus	Copper	Sapphire	Aries
8	Scorpio	Scorpion	Water	Pluto	Plutonium	Jasper	Taurus
9	Sagittarius	Archer	Fire	Jupiter	Tin	Topaz	Gemini
10	Capricorn	Goat	Earth	Saturn	Lead	Black Onyx	Cancer
11	Aquarius	Waterbearer	Air	Uranus	Uranium	Amethyst	Leo
12	Pisces	Fishes	Water	Neptune	Tin	Moonstone	Virgo